"Be the Magic is a powerful and delightful guide
to living with greater joy and purpose in your life.
Diane Pienta pours out equal parts wisdom and love
and offers you fresh ways to experience the magic all around you.
This is a wonderful book you'll want to
come back to again and again."

—MARCI SHIMOFF,
#1 *NY Times* bestselling author,
Happy for No Reason and *Chicken Soup for the Woman's Soul*

Be the
Magic

Bite-Sized Nuggets
of Wisdom to Feed your Joy,
Nourish your Soul
and Open your Heart

Diane Pienta

This is a work of nonfiction. Nonetheless, some names, identifying details, and personal
characteristics of the individuals involved have been changed. In addition, certain people
who appear in these pages are composites of a number of individuals and their experiences.
The author of this book does not dispense medical advice or prescribe the use of any
technique as a form of treatment for physical, emotional, or medical problems without the
advice of a physician, either directly or indirectly. The intent of the author is only to offer
information of a general nature to help you in your quest for well-being. In the event you use
any of the information in the book for yourself, which is your constitutional right,
the author and publisher assume no responsibility for your actions.

With grateful acknowledgment to Coleman Barks and Martín Prechtel for permission to
reprint the following texts in whole and in part, respectively:
Jalal al-Din Rumi, *The Guest House,* in *The Essential Rumi,* trans. Coleman Barks
(San Francisco: Harper Collins, 2002).
Martín Prechtel, *Rescuing the Light: Quotes from the Oral Teachings of Martín Prechtel*
(Berkeley: North Atlantic Books, 2021), Martín Prechtel, Bolad's Kitchen Teaching, 2018.

Library of Congress Cataloging-in-Publication Data • Control Number: 2022921283
Pienta, Diane • *Be the Magic: Bite-Sized Nuggets of Wisdom to Feed your Joy,
Nourish your Soul and Open your Heart*

p. cm.
First Edition, February 2023 • Printed in Canada
Paperback ISBN: 978-1-954569-72-0 • Ebook ISBN: 978-1-954569-27-0
Interior and Cover design by: Mary Ann Casler-Brecher • www.worddesignservices.com

Ⓒ CITRINE PUBLISHING
For information about special discounts for group purchases, please call
+1-828-585-7030 or email Sales@CitrinePublishing.com.

2 3 4 5 6 7 8 9 10

This book is dedicated to the seekers among us
who love the magic and mystery of this awesome world.

Contents

If you can see the magic,

You can be the magic.

If you can be the magic,

You can share the magic.

If you can share the magic,

Your life is blessed beyond measure.

A Few Words To Begin

Walk Softly
Speak Slowly
Carry Flowers
And Stardust

Do you want more magic in your life? Do you want more of that excited yet contented feeling when you wake up in the morning, curious to see what wonders the world has in store for you today?

As I write this, there's a pandemic in full swing, inflation is the highest it's been in fifty years, and there's a war in Europe that many fear is the beginning of World War III. There's not a whole lot of harmony and cooperation in politics and then, there's climate change. Some say that magic has gone a-missing these days.

We might consider that the outer world is simply reflecting our inner state of mind.

Maybe you are a happy, peaceful person, and, maybe your inner landscape is also forested with anxiety, turmoil or apathy. Although we want to live happy, purposeful, creative lives, our hearts and minds can be so darn turbulent.

And yet, the world never stops sending us guidance, nudges, and bricks-over-the head towards what our hearts are longing for, for what would bring us the most joy. If we could just remove the blinders from our eyes, we could attune to the guidance and the beauty…we could see the magic.

Einstein tells us we can't solve a problem with the same level of consciousness we used to create the obstacle in the first place. So, if we want to remove the blinders, if we want our hearts and our world to be joyful, we need to develop a new level of consciousness—and fast…seeing with new eyes, hearing with new ears, speaking and thinking in new ways. I propose that we can do this with ease, and yes, friends, even fun.

Maybe you're now asking yourself some of the age-old questions that have been asked for millennia—Who am I? What am I here to do? What's my truth? How can I be a positive part of the larger picture?

They're part of the human experience, independent of ethnicity, race, gender, or political leanings. And they're infinitely more difficult to answer when we're engaged in negative thinking.

It's been said that teachers teach what they need to learn, and writers write what they need to hear. This book is no exception.

I was one of those highly intuitive children, tapped into the energy of people, situations, places. And, I had a mother who routinely engaged in negative thinking and speaking; a person who consistently replayed hurtful scenarios and ruminated on comments, regrets and mistakes like a skipping record.

We all do this to some degree, and, there are extreme examples like my mother who most likely endured undiagnosed depression or other contributing illness. She lived in a time and place where even admitting you needed help with this was unthinkable. The self-help movement was just an embryo and for my Depression-era, WWII generation parents, it was all woo-woo stuff. You just put your head down, powered through your difficulties and "got on with it."

I watched what happened when she'd spiral into negativity, as thick black clouds filled the house. Joy and Happiness would make a quick beeline for the door, no one in the house was happy, and the good, the beautiful and the magical was invisible to her.

I came into this world hard-wired as a fixer and a pleaser, and so, my gifts of observation and intuition got finely honed as I watched for when the dark clouds would start gathering and found ways to interrupt the storm. Kids are smart, no? When I look back, I realize that I was intuitively exercising many of the practices science is now validating as effective methods for changing our brain patterns.

Naturally upbeat, I would turn on some music that my mother loved and get her to sing or dance with me, ask her to play a game that she enjoyed, talk about how much I liked the flowers in the garden—"Do you like the flowers, too?" I asked her to tell me about her own mother, whom she loved, asked her about her grandparents' farm, which she cherished, generating upbeat positive energy to counteract the negativity. It was often exhausting. It didn't always work, but many times it did.

Though I couldn't know then that happiness is an inside job, I could see that redirecting her thinking towards people and places she loved or appreciated, getting her to move her body in new ways, or moving her from monologue to dialogue had the ability to shift her thoughts toward the light. And if her thoughts shifted toward the light, she could see the magic in life again.

Yet, as happens with habits and patterns, my mother's only got more ingrained and persistent as she grew older. By the time she was seventy, it was nearly impossible to redirect her, and she spent much of the next twenty years in deep negativity, distrust, and disconnectedness as she slipped into dementia.

As many of us are wont to do, I declared early on that I was *never* going to be like my mother!

I could clearly see that people, including myself, would rather be around an upbeat person than a downbeat one. I could see that those people who consistently looked for the good were more engaged, creative, fun and energizing to be around. They laughed a lot more. They had more friends. They often seemed to be fulfilling a purpose greater than just existing. I wanted to be one of those people.

So you might imagine my absolute horror in my early thirties when I suddenly realized that I was ruminating—playing and replaying hurtful scenarios in my mind, anticipating negative reactions, focusing on what wasn't working instead of what was.

Just like my mother.

What I didn't realize back then is that all of us do this to some degree. I didn't understand that many of our patterns are trained into us as small children, whether we like them or not. I just thought I had inherited some really unfortunate genes.

My first generation, non-college-educated parents impressed upon me from an early age that one went to college to "get a good job"—in other words, to make money. My father was a highly creative and skilled craftsman but he traded that dream for a pension and a good benefit package. The money trumped. It seemed to me that "getting a good job" was a ticket out of a Pennsylvania coal-mining town and away from my mother's ranting negativity. I embraced the aspiration whole-heartedly, chalking up an Ivy League degree, a management track with a luxury hotel chain, a stint with a small consulting firm before creating my own, and later a career in real estate. They paid the bills handsomely, though they demanded regular withdrawals from my soul.

As an adult, I lived a double life. The majority of the time, I was a successful business-person, but a cancer diagnosis in my early thirties shook me awake enough to get curious, really curious, about alternative healing modalities, herbal medicine, the power of nature to heal and the power of our thoughts to determine our life. This life suddenly seemed so precious, so fleeting, and our world seemed so incredibly beautiful and magical. I wanted to be a person who recognized this every day, not someone who held onto old conversations and regrets, focusing on "what's wrong." As my mind kept the wheels of business spinning, my heart kept the magic alive by squeezing in positive psychology, creativity, dance, music, art and herbology wherever possible. That, and regular howling at the moon.

And so, after twenty-five years of business, as my father was dying and my mother was spiraling into hard-core dementia, both of them vehemently denying they needed any help, I returned to my hometown to help in whatever ways I could, in what I've come to call the "Death, Dying and Dementia years." The tumultuous negativity of my childhood looked like a picnic compared to this scene, but despite the tears, the fist-shaking at the universe, and the impossible-seeming insanity, I didn't regret my choice when it was over.

In fact, it created an empty space to fill. With my parents gone, no children and a work hiatus, the volume was now turned up on the questions I'd been demanding the Divine to answer…"What's my purpose? What and who was I here to serve?" Telling myself I'd give myself a few months, "a sabbatical," to explore art, spiritual philosophies, healing modalities and the world, seven years passed in a flash as I studied consciousness and energy-based healing, immersed my soul in creativity and music, devoured books and apprenticed with extraordinary teachers.

Do you ever hear exactly what you need to hear, exactly when you need to hear it?

Once I opened myself up to receiving this kind of wisdom, the guidance flowed in—from conversations with random strangers, utterances from wise friends, quotes from beloved teachers or insights that slipped out of my own pen, often when beseeching the clouds for answers.

Curating these particularly poignant quotes into a journal, the book you now hold in your hand grew from those seeds that I collected over the years. And just as the lotus flower grows from the mud, my mother gifted me a few gems through her struggles, mainly a keenly attuned perception of the energy and people around me, a powerful curiosity about how our thoughts shape our lives and a love for peace. These gifts have powered my search for joy in this life, and this book is a collection of mementos gathered on that journey.

Be the Magic is a companion for those of us who want to be in love with life itself, regardless of what's happening in the world. It's for those of us who want to jump out of bed in the morning with enthusiasm and curiosity.

These are vignettes of nourishing wisdom for when you need a wholesome snack to remind you who you really are and to help replace bleak thoughts with bright ones. They're a collection of uplifting and actionable daily practices designed to train our bodies, minds and hearts to become so sweetly attuned to the guidance and magic that is being presented to us in every moment, offering you, the reader, some playful ways to discover your own joy, so that you too can Be the Magic.

The practices in this book can be viewed as games we can play to help pacify our internal wars and allow us to be the eye of the storm, as the storm of life may rage around with a fury. Even now, after decades of working with these practices, I'll randomly turn to a page and find exactly the wisdom I need to make me smile, shift me into awe, or bestow clarity on a murky situation. And sometimes, they just make me laugh at myself for how seriously I can take this life, which honestly is going to be gone in a blink of an eye.

At face value, these might seem like simple practices and stories. Don't let their simplicity deceive you. They are simple yet profound—if you take time to do them.

I hope they'll help you thrive.

• • •

You might read this book all the way through at once.

You might take a story each day or each week and practice it to see what it shifts for you.

You might flip to a random page to see which story wants to connect with you.

Some of the stories are facets of the same story, just as we look at different aspects of our life through different lenses at different times.

However you read this book, I invite you to pause at the end of each vignette and try the practice. See what works and what doesn't. Play. Have fun. What do you have to lose?

It seems that we can all use a helping hand these days to remember what magnificent beings we are, that the world is an awe-inspiring, majestic place, and that when we (with plenty of help from our friends and the heavens!) can see all the magic around us, we can Be the Magic. The more we play and remind each other how to reach for joy, the easier it becomes and the more it spreads.

Do you want to play in this sandbox with me?

May you see all of the magic constantly zooming its way towards you, as you shine your own beautiful light and magic in this magnificent world. You are not alone!

From my heart to yours,

Diane

"She Decided To Stop Looking for The Light and Instead, Become It."

—FRANCHESKA

This book began a few years ago without my realizing it when a quote found me: "She decided to stop looking for the light, and instead, become it."

One thousand thanks to the unknown author of that quote, as it reset the course of my life. Some attribute it to one "Francheska," and if so, I bow to you, Francheska. As I read it, I saw in a moment how I was looking for love in all the wrong places.

"What is my purpose?" was my constant refrain in those days. "What am I here to do?" I'd ask—demand, really—as I went to yoga and prayed for "fulfilling meaningful life work." I collaged it. I journaled about it. I meditated on it and talked about it. I took workshops about it, had my akashic records read about it, and asked my astrologer for a hint. I looked into my past lives for clues, rendezvoused with psychics, and studied all kinds of different venues looking for "it."

13

Now the equation was turned inside out. What if *we* are the light we're looking for? The peace we want to see in others? The joy and belonging we long to feel in the world? What if the joy is in cultivating our light no matter what we're doing so that we become, in the words of qigong master Chunyi Lin, "love radiators"? What if we are the ones who bring the light, no matter what's happening in the world?

Life just got a whole lot more interesting. And fun.

Every morning, I'd ask for divine guidance on how to be the light that day, for opportunities to be in service to the light. To stop looking outside myself for illumination, guidance, and answers and to be the light myself. Not just as a way of calming the antics in my mind, though it had that effect, but to bring the qualities of light and love to everyone and everything I encountered, no matter the circumstances. It seemed that this would be a pretty joyful way to live and might actually be good for the planet. What if this was my purpose?

Little did I know that tuning into one's own light can set the course for a wild ride and in a lovely twist of fate is actually what leads us to purpose. Each of us has our own unique ember, our own light, fed by what some might call "source," the universe, god, goddess, flying spaghetti monster—take your pick. Start to tend that ember; carefully blow some life-giving air. Add some kindling; you choose the type. Maybe it's picking up your paintbrushes again. Or learning that musical instrument you said you always wanted to try. Singing in the shower. Or on stage. Deepening your spiritual practice. Only you know. But the big light will see that you're ready to burst into flame and will add its own fuel to help make yours as magnificent as possible.

Who would you be if you were the light?

"Jealousy Is a Great Informer.
It Tells You What You Want."

—ELLEN TADD

I had never considered myself a jealous person. In my thirties and forties, it seemed I "had it all." People would tell me they were envious of my life.

So it was a bit of a shock when, after fifteen years of doing yoga and threatening to get my yoga teacher certification but never actually doing it, I noticed myself critiquing other teachers' classes, especially teachers who were newer at the game.

After the tenth time or so of saying, "Sheesh, I could have taught a better class," I was struck by the awareness that I was actually envious. I might have been able to teach a better class, but no one would ever know it, including me. They had taken the leap to go to the training and to put themselves out in the world. I hadn't. I was filled with envy.

Ugh! Self-Awareness!

The same thing started happening with books. I'd read something and think, "God, if this thing can get published, I could probably write a best-seller." Except, besides my morning journal, I wasn't writing anything. I joined a nine-month creativity and transformation course, and it seemed that everyone there was on their way to writing a book. I was jealous. Again.

Julia Cameron of *The Artist's Way*—maven of creative expansion—tells us we're jealous when we're not expressing our own creative gifts in the world, not living the creativity that we've come here to do, and that envy just gets louder the longer we ignore it. It seems so easy—just go and do it, right? But it's not. We have creative blocks of all kinds. The good news is that there are plenty of practices to help us dismantle the blocks and learn how to play again if we choose.

Here's the thing about envy. It creates disconnection. It creates you or me, instead of you and me. When we're living our joy, expressing our own unique creative gifts, and are secure in that knowledge, we look for community and collaboration. Then it's fun to encourage and support others in their craft and creativity. We're not threatened. But do you ever notice that the people who are your naysayers, or are at best unsupportive, aren't pursuing their own creativity?

Are you jealous of something?

Become friends with envy. She'll tell you what's missing and maybe even show you where you can find it.

"Jealousy will either kill you or motivate you like nothing else."

—HAZEL HIRA OZBEK

Don't Try So Hard

In my first years of alternative healing explorations, I was still a type-A, make-it-happen kind of person. There was a lot of action orientation, you could say.

One day I saw a flyer for Feldenkrais, a bodywork methodology that reorganizes connections between the brain and the body, improving both body movement and psychological states. I liked the way the name sounded in my mouth, and I found a practitioner. Serenity was her name, and she was my polar opposite. Slow and soft spoken, with loose drapey clothing, she was gentle and calm to the point I wanted to ask her to "get on with it." I think I might have been expecting a vigorous massage or maybe a lengthy diagnosis of my body.

After an hour on the table with Serenity moving my hands and fingers almost imperceptibly, barely touching me, she said we were done and commented dreamily, "I noticed you clench your hands a *lot*. Pay attention to that." WHAT? I had driven across town in thick traffic and paid $150 to be told I clench my fists? So what? "A waste of money," I thought. Check Feldenkrais off the list.

But her words somehow lodged themselves in my consciousness, and I kept noticing how my hands were very often clenched in fists, like …what? I was ready to defend? To fight? I even woke up with clenched fists. I was tense. Tight. I had somehow convinced myself that I was so relaxed from all the yoga I did. But the body doesn't lie.

I eventually forgot all about Feldenkrais and clenched fists until a few years ago when I was studying Eastern European fiddle with musical genius Beth Bahia Cohen. One day, Beth exclaimed, "What are you doing, grasping your instrument in a death grip?! Your hands are clenched on the neck! It's like anything in life: you hold it as lightly as you can without dropping it!"

I thought back to yoga classes where I went in so tired that I had no choice but to give myself a break, to tell myself to not have any expectations and that I'd be in child's pose most of the time. Without fail, those classes were the deepest, easiest, most balanced classes. I would balance rock steady in tree pose, lift effortlessly in dancer's pose.

In the words of wise woman Mary Morrissey, "Give up the pretense that by being tense you can make something better."

Where are you trying a little too hard right now? Where are you holding tension in your body? Maybe in a death grip? Your jaw? Your hands? Your shoulders? Maybe you're holding a part of your life that you feel you've got to "power through" and "make something happen."

What happens if you relax your hands, drop your shoulders? What happens if you smile right now? What happens if you hold your life as lightly as you can without dropping it?

Two Women with a Map,

Do you ever experience that the universe provides exactly what you need, exactly when you need it? Not before or after, but exactly at the right time?

A few years ago, I went for a walk in the Blue Hills Reservation just outside Boston. Original home to the Nipmuc and Wampanoag peoples, with seven thousand mostly undeveloped acres, one might be able to imagine what this land was like before the colonists arrived.

I never took a map when I walked the reservation, despite its large swath and 125 miles of trails. "It's practically in the city!" I thought. I mean, you can hear the highways from a lot of the trails. Plus, I'd always prided myself on my sense of direction and "inner radar." It would be impossible for me to get lost.

That particular day, I walked for two hours without seeing a single person and was headed back to the car. Or so I thought. I'd left my cell phone in the car so I wouldn't be text-tempted and was feeling lovingly connected with the land and the trails. Until I wasn't.

Suddenly, nothing looked familiar. The sky had just turned deep overcast, and I couldn't get a good sense of where the sun was to align my direction. I turned around and walked back. And then did it again. And again. And realized I was going in circles.

I tried to hear the highway to orient myself, but the wind was playing tricks on me. I'd never been lost in the woods, and while I knew this was not deep wilderness, I was by myself in what seemed like an oncoming cold thunderstorm and was disoriented enough to get anxious.

Collecting myself, I stood still, and with eyes closed and breathing deeply, I asked the universe, "Which way do I go? Point me in the right direction to get me home safely."

I felt a tug to my left, then hesitated, as left didn't feel accurate. Recalling a friend who would ask my advice then argue with my response, I figured if I wasn't going to listen to the answer, I shouldn't have asked the question! So left I went.

Within a few minutes, I started hearing voices—two women jabbering loudly and animatedly—the only people I'd encountered in two hours. "It's this way!" I heard. "No, that's not right. Get out the map!" the other demanded. The women seemed as surprised to see me as I was to see them. Relief washed over me as I looked over their map and got my bearings.

"Where's your map?!" the bossy one interrogated me. "You're the first person we've seen in hours. What are you doing without a map?"

They'd just taken a wrong turn minutes before. At precisely the same time, I'd asked the universe for directions. If I'd run into them fifteen minutes earlier, I wouldn't have known I needed the map. If they'd not taken a wrong turn exactly when they did, our paths wouldn't have crossed. We met, the three of us, in the midst of seven thousand acres at exactly the right place and moment. I got exactly what I needed at exactly the right time, not before or after.

I try to remember this when I'm confused and searching for answers, when I'm feeling disoriented or lost in life, going around in circles, unsure what direction to take. The formula is simple; it's just the trust that can throw us for a loop.

1. *Get quiet.* It can be hard to soften your mind when you're feeling anxious. I know! You can try gently blurring your eyes, taking some deep breaths, and finding a point to lightly focus your eyes on.

2. *Ask a direct question.* The more specific you can be, the easier it is for the universe to answer you.

3. *Wait for the answer.* Can you relax while you wait for the answer and trust that it will come? Waiting for an answer in such circumstances can be a bit tricky. It's a soft but vigilant waiting that's needed. You have to relax while you wait for the answer and trust that it will come. Some times it takes a while. Can you take your mind off the question while the universe arranges things behind the scenes for you?

4. *Follow the breadcrumbs,* even when your mind or your ego thinks it knows better.

5. *Find magic and directions to appropriate action.* Two women with a map, exactly *when* I need them, exactly *where* I need them. Can you think of a time when you were provided with exactly what you needed and couldn't have planned it more perfectly if you'd tried? Is there something today you could put that kind of trust in?

*"Focus on What's Changing,
Not What's Staying The Same."*

—JERROD KERR

I was on the phone with my friend Jerrod when I broke my ankle. I was in the park, and I knew that the injury was serious as soon as it happened. How would I get home a mile away? "Oh this is bad!" I yelped. "Please send some gold light or whatever flavor of positive energy or prayer you do."

Unbeknownst to me, Jerrod was trained in a type of energetic healing, and as he worked on me remotely, he repeated in his soothing voice, "Focus on what's changing, not what's staying the same." Over and over he chanted until my mind was focused and actually curious and totally in tune with what was shifting by the moment. I was suddenly engaged in a deep relationship with my ankle.

Instead of focusing on the trauma—"Oh my God! I think I broke my ankle! How am I going to get home? This really hurts! How could

I have done this?!"—I got calmly curious about how the pain was shifting, if it was increasing or decreasing, and I swear, it just started to hurt less. Wanting it to be better, I looked for the improvement and focused on that instead of the damage. I was much more engaged with my ankle itself than in the upset over the accident.

I ask this question now when my life seems stagnant, when it feels like nothing's happening toward my goals, or when I'm worried about something. The question somehow leads us to focus on almost imperceptible shifts and guides us to look for what's improving. It's a great trick.

Where can you focus on what's changing instead of what's staying the same?

The "What If" Game

In Mariem Pérez Riera's 2021 documentary film, *Rita Moreno: Just a Girl Who Decided to Go for It*, the stage and screen icon talks about how actors play the "what if" game. Scholar/practitioner of ancient mystery traditions Marguerite Rigoglioso is a master at this game, too.

Here's how you play. You take a situation that's causing you some agita. Say you're going to a particular family member's house for dinner, an encounter you've come to dread. You just know it's not going to be particularly fun, so you plan on putting your head down to get through it with as little brain damage as possible.

But wait! What if!? What if you started thinking of the visit as fun? Pleasant? Easygoing? Enjoyable? Relaxing? Full of love and connection? What if you started imagining how it would feel to have an easy, loving time and then started acting that way? I know. You're about to say, "You don't know MY family." But what if you just played the game?

Say you're dreading the chore of cleaning out the basement. You know you "should" do it, but you feel like it's going to be really hard and anxiety provoking and, well, just not fun. But WHAT IF?! What if you took a moment to ask yourself, "What if this is going to be easy? What if I'm going to find all kinds of interesting things? What if this could be . . . fun?" What if you started imagining how satisfying it was going to be? How would you approach it if you knew it was going to be enjoyable?

Or you can be like Marguerite and play big. Marguerite's What If games include things like "What if everyone in the world perceived life through their third eye (higher consciousness) instead of their solar plexus (emotional reaction)?" What if we all took a moment to imagine what the world would be like if every person (including you!) had all the love they needed, so they didn't respond to others from a stressed or hurt place, and operated from a higher perspective?

Imagination is powerful. Your thoughts are incredibly powerful.

Thoughts affect every cell and organ of our bodies. I often imagine my thoughts as a pitcher of liquid being poured into the top of my head and spreading to every single cell and organ inside. When I start to think dark or negative thoughts about myself or others, if I'm lucky I catch myself and think, "Oh, poor cells, being flushed with toxic, unhappy, negative, worrisome thoughts." I would not be happy if someone else poured a whole pitcher of toxicity over me. So why did I just do it to myself? I pick up another pitcher of uplifting golden thoughts and take a shower in that.

What do you want to fill your whole body up with? What would feel most delicious to you? Be good to yourself. See what happens.

What if you filled yourself with juicy, loving, zesty, vital, fun-loving thoughts? What if they had the power to move your life in that direction?

There's only one way to find out.

Listen for, and expect miracles.

See The Magic. Be The Magic.

Not long ago, my husband, Dave, and I sold our house without having another. Maybe I was reading too much Zen spiritual material, the ones that tell you "Jump! And the net will appear!" But shortly thereafter, our temporary housing evaporated at a moment's notice, and we were wondering when exactly that net was going to appear. Seemed we needed to weave one, and so in a fit of inspiration, we bought a camper van, christened her *Serenity Rose the Motor Om*, and set out to explore this magnificent world for a magical new place where we could settle and contribute our gifts.

The most common response we got to our story was, "Oh man, that is *so cool*." But we didn't feel cool. We felt decidedly ungrounded and a little shaken. And when the best of us are ungrounded and shaken, it's easy to fall into fear and negativity. I started a blog as a way to stay tethered to our community (and to not fall into despair) and decided that my job now was to look and see magic everywhere and to share it.

Now it was cool. Traveling without a plan, following the magic crumbs of synchronicity, we stayed on farms and vineyards (aka boondocking). We were immersed in nature and connecting with inspiring people who were expressing their creativity on the land and sharing it with others. We kept calling to the land and were eager to see where and when it would lead to home.

And then winter approached. We hadn't found any place that called to us. The breadcrumbs had seemingly blown away, and we found ourselves . . . back in Boston. We needed a home base and turned to an investment apartment we had owned for decades that was now coincidentally vacant. It was in the heart of the city, practically in the middle of the Boston University campus near the hospital district, with its constant barrage of students and sirens and traffic. We're talking Times Square loud. I'd always said I would never live there. Never ever. I'm an über-Virgo who needs to be surrounded by grass and gardens, fresh air and sky, but somehow, there we were, moving into this city apartment.

This seemed like some kind of mean cosmic joke. Where was that freaking net, anyway?

After months of sleeping outdoors, under the stars and the moon, with the coyotes and deer, awakened by birdsong, I steeled myself for the onslaught of urban humanity and wondered how best to survive the assault.

Turns out, the best way was to decide that my job was still to look and see the magic everywhere. I walked out the front door and asked, "Please lead me to some magic." My feet started moving, and in a few minutes, I found myself in Longwood Mall, a two-and-a-half-acre park with historic beech trees, thought to be the oldest grove of European beech in the United States. How could I have lived in Boston for thirty years and never seen this? They were so magnificent and literally welcomed me with open arms and deep roots. The next morning unveiled an ancient cedar swamp four blocks in the opposite direction.

There was an organic market two blocks from the house, good restaurants, and a robust and welcoming yoga community. The beautiful Muddy River winds through the neighborhood, and the great blue herons and migratory birds that gather there fly parallel to the diesel trucks and ambulances on the adjacent Riverway. Stepping out for an evening walk, the stars were obscured with the light pollution from Fenway stadium, but the energy of the neighborhood was alive and vibrant and creative—and fun. The fervor of the Red Sox game spilled into the streets, and the students' youthful vibrancy was stimulating. We looked at each other in surprise, agreeing that it seemed like we just moved into a really interesting European city.

Life sometimes gives us just what we need when we're looking in the opposite direction, no?

What we appreciate, appreciates. Appreciating the magic begets more magic. Appreciating what's wonderful trains our brains to look for what's good instead of what's not. Focusing on what doesn't work just gets more of what doesn't work.

There's magic everywhere when we open our hearts to it.

What magic is in your life today? What if you filled the margins with it?

Don't Be Afraid of The Silence

I was in the kitchen at Mountain Light Sanctuary, deep in the Great Smoky Mountains of North Carolina, a magical piece of land with rustic dwellings where one can easily get divebombed by hummingbirds and blue butterflies, where wild rhododendrons grace the edges of moss-lined streams full of fairy pools and waterfalls. It's a place where nature speaks delicious, caressing, soul-satisfying phrases 24/7 with her rushing streams, rustling bamboo groves, trilling birdsong, and a million other echoes. To hear that kind of transmission is beyond awe-inspiring—and requires a quiet, gentle silence on our part.

Do you ever notice that our modern culture has a problem with silence?

Silence has become almost taboo as we reach instinctively for our devices to constantly fill our ears with music, news, and podcasts.

Never was this more obvious than in the kitchen at Mountain Light Sanctuary that day. Another guest was making lunch, speaking virtually nonstop. She barely took a breath as her speech flitted like a bee, yakking in intricate detail about how she was going to cook her spaghetti squash, how tired she was, how much she loved Mountain Light, how hard it was to make time to go there, how she was going to pick some apples from the tree, and on and on and on with no space for dialogue or even a moment's pause, oblivious to the LARGE sign in the pantry:

> *Before you speak, consider …*
> *Is it necessary?*
> *Is it kind?*
> *Is it an improvement upon the silence?*
> *If you can't improve upon the silence, please don't break it.*

Mountain Light is the kind of place where one might ask oneself, "What is this annoyance trying to teach me?" instead of having a thought bubble that says, "This woman is so F#*&ing annoying! I wish she'd shut up! Get me out of here!"

Yes, I know. It would be infinitely easier to stick with "She is so F#*&ing annoying." But I was chasing that Zen place where I could be with someone like that and have no annoyance whatsoever, so I figured I had to ask myself the question.

The answer came, reminding me that social anxiety is more the norm than the exception in our society. It taught me to have compassion for someone who feels such an obsessive compulsion to express themselves nonstop and maybe can't help it. It spotlighted how draining it can be to be in the presence of that kind of incessant rambling. And it taught me that I, too, fill silences instead of letting silences be, that for most of us, letting silence be is an art we haven't been taught. We've been taught that the loudest one wins.

And then I thought, "Holy crap! Is this what it's like for the forest when I'm sitting there with my mind going a million miles a second?" Even though I don't often talk aloud in the forest, Robin Wall Kimmerer tells us in her magical book *Braiding Sweetgrass* that the trees can sense our energy, whether our thoughts are calm and peaceful or frenetic and whirring. Are the trees saying about my presence, "This woman is so annoying with her nonstop head chatter, I wish she'd be quiet"? Well, that was something to contemplate.

I don't suggest for a second that we all walk around in silence. Eloquence is one of the highest arts, a gorgeous way we connect, create, and collaborate. Finding and using our voice in inspired action and speech is critical to our well-being and to our genuine participation in this world. It's how we stay connected with family and friends—and life. Life happens in conversations. As birds sing back and forth to each other, our speech is our birdsong. I mean, I'm talking a lot in this book right now.

So maybe the questions are: Are we energizing others, ourselves, the world with our speech? Do we think about its impact and how others are affected by how and what we say? Do we care how people are left after being in our presence? Can we be comfortable with silence long enough to wait and see what truly wants to be said?

I'll be quiet now.

What's your relationship to silence?

"Listen to silence. It has so much to say." —JALAL AL-DIN RUMI

Getting Started Is The Hardest Part

A few years ago, I was lucky enough to be included with a group of people re-mudding a beloved and sacred southwestern adobe building, built in the original straw, mud, water method. We were there to give this hall a fresh coat of "mud," just the right kind of dirt mixed with just the right amount of finely ground straw and water.

Like many of the others, I'd never done this and was learning from a beautiful man considered the best and foremost expert on repairing and restoring the old historic adobe churches in the Southwest. I was excited. And a little nervous.

He started our instructions. "Get yourself a bucket of mud and maybe a trowel." I was ready for elaborate instruction on how to trowel a smooth finish, nervously hoping my work would be good enough for this special building. I figured we'd have a few hours of instructions and then be allowed to practice somewhere.

Our teacher walked over to the wall, plunged his forearm deep in the mud bucket, and slapped it on the wall, smoothing it around with the palm of his hand. He looked at the trowel and tossed it aside. He did this twice more, then said, "That's how you do it. Go ahead; you'll figure it out."

The small group of us hesitated. Responding to our questioning looks of surprise, he said, "It's like so many things in life. The hardest part is getting started. You just have to get in and do it."

I thought of how many times I'd put off doing something I wasn't skilled in because of not getting it right, or thinking I needed a *lot* more preparation and education. Here was a master craftsperson setting us loose on a sacred building, whose instruction amounted to little more than "Just do it and figure it out." Friends, this is a joyful way to live.

Is there something you're delaying that you can start now? Just put your hand in and feel the mud. You can do it. Your soul wants you to start.

"A journey of a thousand miles starts with a single step." —LAOZI

Keep Your Eye upon The Donut

*"As you travel on through life, let this always be your goal.
Keep your eye upon the donut, and not upon the hole."*

—FRANK PIENTA

When I was seven, I was given an "autograph book." Autograph books were a thing in the 70s, and I went around, asking people to sign it. My mother, who kept everything, tucked it away, and forty-plus years later, it surfaced, along with all the advice offered to me by the adults of my childhood world.

This one stood the test of time. I hadn't thought of my father as a positive psychologist, but what better encouragement can we give each other than to focus on what we *do* want, not what we *don't* want, to focus on what's good instead of what's not working, to see and appreciate what we have instead of what we think is missing.

Are you focusing on a hole in your life? Is there a donut that might be more mouthwatering?

Thanks, Dad.

Failure Is Your Friend

"At least if you're failing, you know you're alive; you're participating, engaged, learning, and therefore contributing to evolution. The Japanese have a phrase for this—they call it 'the nobility of failure,' implying, Look at all the great things at which this person failed. She was really alive."

—CAROLINE W. CASEY

Well, Phew! I guess I am really truly alive! Isn't this a fantastic way to try something new? Not, "Will I be successful at this?" but "Do I feel alive!?"

How many times have you heard that there's no mastery without failure—lots of failure? Move toward what gives you joy and peace—discernment is key here. And when you goof up—and you will!—then laugh at yourself for being human, dust yourself off, and try again.

When a child is learning a new skill—how to read, how to write their name, or learn 2 + 2—we don't chastise them when they goof up. We often think the failures are adorable. We tell them they're doing great, and we gently show them how to improve and encourage them to just keep practicing. Even if there are a hundred backward letters for each successful one, we don't stop cheering them on. So as adults, why do we beat ourselves up for our failures instead of saying, "Great try!" "Good job!" "You can do it!"?

You can read any of a thousand books written on this very subject, but all the words and science and reasons won't make you be nicer to yourself when you fail. You just have to start doing it, one step at a time.

Considering failure as a sign of being alive is giving me, well, the aliveness to continue writing this book. Instead of focusing on "What if it's a failure?" and getting locked up at my writing desk, I see myself as an engaged person willing to try something new and scary regardless of the outcome.

I wonder if something in your soul wants to come out and play and be alive—regardless of the outcome.

"Courage doesn't come from ability, ability comes from courage."

—MARTÍN PRECHTEL

Interrupt The Pattern

For the past decade, I've been playing with something I call "interrupting the pattern," consciously choosing to do things differently from my habitual norm. Like taking a new route without GPS, using my non-dominant hand—or in a moment of either bravery or foolhardiness, selling my house without having another. It's all in service of seeing the world through fresh eyes, with wonder and delight.

Wisdom for the Arts, a transformational leadership program guiding its' participants to access their inner wisdom through creativity, explores this idea that we often try to solve a problem by talking about it as opposed to by changing our structures (i.e., behaviors) to get different results. The other day, Dave and I were having a bit of a disagreement. I grabbed my hula hoop and tried to keep the conversation going while I hooped—which made me fall down laughing instead. Discord dissolved!

As the Dalai Lama quips, "I am the source of my own suffering because of the habits of my mind." Doing anything habitually in the same way fosters dullness, as we operate on autopilot. It's easier to appreciate things that are new. And more grateful means more happy. I don't know about you, but I can always use more happy.

Dr. Vimala Rodgers does this "interrupt the pattern" routine, too, through her International Institute of Handwriting Studies. She makes the bold claim that you can change your life by changing your handwriting, by interrupting the pattern of how you've formed your letters for years. I was intrigued and jumped into a six-month course of study with her.

People had always complimented me on my elegant, calligraphy-like handwriting, but as the hand/brain research pioneer that she is, Vimala gently pointed out some of the ways that my letters, habitually formed for decades, could be hindering my creativity and other positive attributes. I was doubtful. And a little curious.

Relearning a new handwriting system is hard. My brain didn't like it. Or maybe my brain liked it and my ego was annoyed. My formerly artistic, praiseworthy handwriting now looked like a seven year old's scribble as my brain tried to make sense of it all.

According to Vimala, each stroke of the Vimala alphabet, based on sacred geometry, is designed to cultivate qualities that enlighten the spirit. Instead of working with our minds, to try to reprogram our brains to be more confident, trusting, creative etc., we can let our hands teach our brains to make the changes we want to see. This seemed like magic to me. And a whole lot more fun. As Vimala says early and often to her students, "Don't believe me. Try it for yourself!"

What can you do today to interrupt the pattern? What if you write a paragraph with your nondominant hand? How can you move your body in an unfamiliar way? Can you say yes to something you usually pooh-pooh?

See if you're not just a little more lighthearted after this.

Your Comfort Zone Will Kill You

And it will do so slowly, like little knives nicking you imperceptibly as you bleed to death unaware. Take it from one who knows.

I like to work and was always a creative, productive person, always had projects going on, groups I was involved with, work to do. Time often seemed short, with never-ending demands, and I'd sometimes fantasize about ditching it all. Clear the decks!

After burning out from too much work combined with years of helping my difficult, elderly parents navigate decline, dementia, and death, I decided to clear the decks completely. I took time for me, which was a wonderful thing, and I settled into a very comfortable and initially fun and fulfilling existence of travel, study, art, and ... comfort.

After being of service to family, work, and community for many years, I shunned anything that would tie me down or make me too responsible, protecting myself from too many demands or extensive commitments while I waited for my life's purpose to reveal itself.

I was addicted to my comfort zone and was very . . . comfortable.

Except. I had this perpetual nagging feeling that I was here to do something more. I wasn't challenging myself in any significant way. I wasn't in any kind of service that was making my heart sing. I had always lived in bright vivid color, and now things were turning a bit sepia.

Write a book? *Don't know how, seems too hard, and what do I have to say, anyway?*

Become a forest therapy guide? *Gosh, the training seems so long, and I'm not getting any younger. How old would I be before I am ready to start a practice, and would the training infringe on my many travel plans?*

Go for a winter walk each night to see the stars? *It's so cold! Maybe tomorrow.*

Try the 6 a.m. yoga? *Oh no. Too early. I'm not a morning person.*

Host big outdoor winter picnics like I used to? *It's so much work to create that. I'm not sure I want to spend days cooking and planning.*

After a couple of years of this, I walked into the house after a consultation with a particularly old and beautiful cherry tree and told my husband that we should sell the house—yes, without having an-other—to see what would happen, that we needed to get out of our comfort zone. He just looked at me quietly. Then he gulped and agreed.

This seemingly crazy act led us to months living on a boat in the Sea of Cortez, which inadvertently led to buying a camper van to live in. This led to my starting a blog out of a desperate fear of swirling off into nomadland, which in turn led to this book you're reading. Seemingly effortlessly, I'm a regular at 6 a.m. yoga, I've just gathered a small group of friends for a winter picnic, and am now a forest therapy guide.

Yes friends, I know this is an extreme example. And there are so many little things we can do to shift the comfort zone. I didn't need to sell the house. I could have started the 6 a.m. yoga practice, immersed myself in training, or just got myself out of the cozy warm house each night. I could have interrupted my pattern of comfort.

Magic happens when you do this.

Julia Cameron urges us, "We are creators. We are born to create. Creation is required of us to feed Life herself." And creation isn't just a one-off thing. Looking back at something we created years ago does nothing to feed life or ourselves today. Often, when we're in our comfort zone, we've stopped creating.

I met a woman at the John C. Campbell Folk School not long ago, an elder who was a master knitter and had taught art her whole life. She showed me a most exquisite, intricate poncho she'd just whipped up. She told me that unless she created something with fiber at least three to four hours a day, she couldn't sleep at night. I suddenly realized that if I didn't write two to three hours a day, *I* couldn't sleep at night. Garrison Keillor shares that he wrote himself out of depression; writing was the only thing that would keep his sleeplessness and depression at bay.

With an estimated seventy million Americans with chronic sleep problems, maybe the sleeplessness is our soul knocking when we can't ignore her, asking us to get out of our comfort zone, pressing us to take the steps to create and do what we love, to do what we came here to do. What if our national sleep crisis could be remedied by following our heart's creative call two to three hours a day? Wouldn't that be something?

My dear friend Kathleen was appalled when she read that last paragraph. A professional with a full-time career and mother of a magical, active seven-year-old, Kathleen exclaimed with a bit of an eye roll, "Really, Diane!? Who has the time to follow their joy two to three hours a day!? I mean, that's just not realistic. Or helpful."

Kathleen has a point. We played with this over breakfast. Tiny steps that inch you toward your goal are often the most effective and sustainable. Maybe ten minutes a day is a more helpful suggestion. And what if we worked toward arranging our lives to spend three less hours doing the things that drag us down and devote them to our joy—three less hours on the computer and social media, three less hours watching mindless television, three less hours complaining to our friends about what we don't like? Kathleen's eyes lit up as a lightbulb went off. She showed me an app on her phone that tracked her screen time. Kathleen is not even remotely ranked as a heavy user of social media or technology, and yet there it was in digital black and white: her app showed that her average daily time on her screen last week was just under three hours.

Imagine jumping out of bed excitedly in the morning, delighted and interested in what the day holds, having our hearts sing. Getting out of our comfort zone can often pave the way there.

What's one thing you'd like to try, to test your comfort zone today?

"The modern world has so much comfort; this is depression's little nest."

—MARTÍN PRECHTEL

Just Three Stitches

Do you have the "productivity gene?" How do you feel about sitting down in the middle of the day to read, whittle, embroider, or the like? Friends, if you do this easily, you are blessed beyond measure. Carry on and turn the page.

If sitting down to embroider in the middle of the day when the to-do list is a mile long and there's work to be done conjures up a sense of guilt bordering on anxiety for you, you're not alone. These are activities I'd relegate to the end of the day, that is, when I was tired and unmotivated and therefore, usually didn't get to them. Or worse: I'd think they were activities you did when you were old and retired and you didn't have anything to do besides watch TV and hope your kids called.

Problem was, magical herbalist and wise woman Kate Gilday had just taught me how to make pine-needle baskets. I loved making pine-needle baskets, but at the end of the day, with eyes tired, I'd fall into bed and promise myself I'd work on them tomorrow.

So I came up with a game I call Just Three Stitches. I told myself that surely, I had time to take three stitches before the workday started. Just three stitches. How long could that take? It would satisfy my craving to sew, and I didn't have to find an hour or even thirty minutes. Just three stitches. Three minutes. Tops.

You can probably guess: there is absolutely no way to do only three stitches once you start. Three stitches turned into ten stitches that turned into "just one more row!" that turned into "Holy cow! I'm going to be late!" But it was no longer a frustrated, "Ugh, I'm going to be late." It was a laughing, dancing, dashing out the door, joy-filled, energized start to the day. Even on days with time for truly just three stitches, delight still came knocking.

It works equally well for things you love as for things you "should be doing," things that have been blinking at you day after day as you think, "I'll get to it." Either way, Just Three Stitches brings joy. And who couldn't use a little more joy right about now?

Want to write a book? Surely you've got time for just three sentences. Want to clean out a closet? Just three items is a good start. Been threatening to start drawing again? How about just three lines? Wish you had time for a yoga class? Just three poses can do the trick.

Where can you play Just Three? What if you tried it now?

"Let The Beauty You Love Be What You Do."
— JALAL AL-DIN RUMI

Two decades ago, this quote of Rumi's became my signature tagline. I was working in real estate at the time, often putting in sixty-plus hours a week. It was not the beauty I loved, but it's what I did. I'm not sure I really understood the quote completely at the time, and maybe I was just trying to be clever, but when a psychic said to me in no uncertain terms, "You just need to find your joy and do it! Just find your F#*&ing joy and do it!!", I felt like she had hit me on the head with a brick.

Rumi's poem begins, "Today, like every other day, we wake up empty and frightened. Don't go to the study and start reading. Take down a musical instrument. And let the beauty you love be what you do." A thousand years ago, Rumi was exhorting us, as he does now, to find our joy and let that be what we do in the world. Now. Today. Paulo Coelho chimes in, "One day you will wake up and there won't be any more time to do the things you've always wanted to do. Do it now."

The late master healer Dr. Pankaj Naram taught that 95% of people don't actually know what they want and that this "not knowing what we want" is what contributes to and causes disease, distress, depression. That helping someone discern what they actually want—what beauty they love—is critical to their healing process.

What do you *want*? What do you *love*?

The reasons for not doing what we love are often insidious old patterns that we don't even realize are running our lives. The stories and the reasons are endless, and we modern people are not conditioned to prioritize our own joy. We're conditioned to prioritize duty and production.

A year into my marriage, my usually generous and very loving mother-in-law loudly declared at a dinner with friends and family that I wasn't a good daughter-in-law because I'd gone on a two-month business trip and "left my husband alone." Thinly veiling my dismay at being publicly called out, I laughed it off, always thinking myself an independent, free-thinking wife, but I left that job shortly after. Years later, I learned of a six-week yoga teacher training in Hawaii. I secretly wanted to go but said to myself, "It's too long to be gone from home." What?! Before and in the early years of marriage, I used to travel seven months a year for work! I had no children to take care of, just a husband who was more than capable of fending for himself. I didn't even realize this record was now running the show. But being a "good wife" was now subconsciously more important than pursuing my own joy.

Finding our joy doesn't have to be a huge undertaking, nor do we need to run to the ashram for six weeks to do it. Maybe it's clearing your schedule and getting your sewing machine out for the afternoon, or your woodworking tools. Maybe it's taking the class you've been eyeing. You don't have to quit your job today and become a poet. Although you could.

Trust that even the smallest step in the direction of your joy will lead you home to yourself and please your heart and the gods beyond measure.

Is something keeping you from letting the beauty you love be what you do? What do you love?

"Keep knocking, and the joy inside will eventually open a window to see who's there." —JALAL AL-DIN RUMI

Don't Wait for Perfection. Just Get in the Game.

Don't wait for perfection to step on the court. It's not coming, it won't. There's only today, this moment, this *now*. Step into your game, what will be revealed is *how*.

I admit, I'm talking to myself here. A self-professed perfectionist, I know all too well how, in the words of renowned positive psychologist Tal Ben Shahar, "perfection is the enemy of the good."

If I followed my own advice, I'd stop proofing and editing this little book a hundred more times until it's elusively "perfect," bless it, and get it out the door. A good-enough completed book is better than one that sits on the desk waiting to be perfect.

And yet. A good friend recently challenged me on this notion that perfection herself is the issue. Invoking Frederico García Lorca's concept of *duende* as an antidote to a stilted concept of perfection, my provocateur contended that one might well argue that life is too short *not* to fight tooth and nail, fully and hotly, to squeeze every drop of juice from our particular fruit, to invite, coax, and cajole the life-force to surge up in us. It is the abstract—and so limiting!—ideal of *being* perfect, he proposed, that disengages us from the wonderful, gnarly struggle to bring forth that one special shade of fabric, that perfect phrase, that gesture that will allow the quilt or the song or the dance to come to life—the "Aha!" moment that ignites the project.

Can we pour our absolute heart and soul into our craft, our work, our dream, approach it with a kind of gusto like our life depends on it, infused with the juiciest of vitality, and give up the chase for our own private perfection? Do you hold back on yourself or your projects because you're "not ready yet?"—thinking your art or your service isn't good enough yet? Maybe you think you just need one more class, one more certification, more practice painting or playing your instrument or sewing before you share it with the world.

This modern world of ours dangles the elusive prize of perfection everywhere we look—sixty-year-old women with glowing unwrinkled skin, celebrities who seem effortlessly to have the perfect life, people who seem to be flawlessly executing their craft. Vulnerability, mistakes, and "good enough" seem to be extinct. Does this seem weird to you?

Two years ago, I was suddenly jolted out of my perfection reverie by a friend who asked when I was going to start using and contributing my rapidly accumulating healing skills in the world. Well, I was waiting to "perfect" those skills and teachings before sharing. Read: I was scared.

In the words of Reid Hoffman, founder of LinkedIn, "If you're not embarrassed by the first version of your product, you've launched too late." The idea of perfection can paralyze us into inaction. Inaction can steal confidence. And lack of confidence makes us believe we or our gift aren't good enough yet, which loops us back into inaction. A nasty cycle.

Is the only way, in the simple and clichéd words of Nike, to "Just do it!"? Sort of. But with the twist: add discernment. How to do this? By trusting your heart instead of listening to your head. Your mind will tell you you're not ready yet or not good enough yet, but if you can make friends with your heart, she'll whisper the next step to take and assure you when you are absolutely ready to roll. Your heart will make sure your actions are aligned with your spirit.

And here's the thing: we don't have to know how to do it. In fact, most times, we don't have any idea how to do something. We just need to take the next logical step, and then the next logical step, trusting the doors that open and thanking those that close.

When my father was dying and my mother was spiraling into deep dementia, both of them living in the same house they'd lived in together for sixty-five years and vehemently denying that they needed any help, I was beside myself. I worried about how the final years would look and if there'd be enough money to cover the care that was needed. Would I have to use my own retirement savings to help them? Would my mother let anyone inside the house without claiming they were stealing the bags of frozen broccoli?

This need for "knowing"—aka "getting it right"—was paralyzing. I don't know about you, but I find it pretty hard to access magical synchronistic miracles when I'm all locked up in fear of not getting it right.

The books and well-meaning friends' advice rang hollow. I went to see a rock-star intuitive to see if I could get some help from another realm. Immediately, my long-dead grandmother came in and had just one thing to say: "You are worrying way too much! It's all going to work out. You don't need to know *how* it's all going to work out, you just need to take the next step. And then after that, you'll know the next step, and then the next." She was right. My parents' final years were nothing like I imagined they would be. Caregivers materialized as though from thin air, and my Depression-era mother had somehow secretly stashed away enough money to cover all of it. Unforeseen challenges reared their heads, too, but I couldn't have anticipated those, either.

I'm sitting in a grove of two-hundred-year-old beech trees as I write this. Each has given its all to being the most magnificent beech tree it can be. The beauty of these trees is how they're twisted and gnarled, in their broken, regenerating forms. This very "imperfection" is what makes them interesting. No worrying here if they're ready or if they look just right; they're just lifting toward the light, just being their perfectly imperfect selves.

Is there somewhere you've been holding back, waiting to perfect yourself before you share yourself with the world? Or maybe waiting to figure out "how?"

Can you consider that maybe you're ready right now?

Is there one little step you can take today, just one, that moves your already perfect self into the ring?

How charming that the word *imperfect* so easily becomes *I'm perfect*.

Climb More Trees

When I was little, I loved to climb trees. An old cherry tree in our backyard was my favorite. I'd climb about fifteen feet up—which when you're seven feels like skyscraper height—dangle from branch to branch, and mostly just hang out. I'd spy on the neighbors, scare my mother when she came out to hang laundry, and get eye-to-eye with the flaky maroon bark, picking at it, rubbing it.

Life didn't get much happier for me than when I was up in that tree (although dancing in the living room to "American Woman" was a close second).

Forty years later, looking for purpose and answers to life's usual questions, I picked up my pen and wrote, "What do I need to know right now?" The answer shot straight through the arrow of my pen, hitting the bulls-eye. My pen wrote, "Climb more trees." Huh?

I hadn't climbed a tree in forty years. What kind of advice was this?

Sometimes there are signs. The next day, our neighbors had a backyard cookout. And it just so happened that one of the guests was a tree climber—as in, he climbs to the crowns of trees for fun and teaches others to do this with ropes and saddles. He pointed to the grand oak tree across the yard and said, "That one is *perfect* for climbing."

When the universe delivers, I try my best to just say "Hey, thanks," and so the next day, I got into a saddle and spent hours in this magnificent tree. Andrew talked about the phenomenon called "tree time," where time passes at a completely different pace. You'd think you were in a tree for fifteen or twenty minutes, look at your watch, and wonder if it could be correct that three hours had passed. A kind of Rip Van Winkle effect.

I had a sudden memory of my mother asking what I did "up in that tree for hours." Confused, I'd tell her I was there for just a couple of minutes. But the experience, both then and now, is the same—my head was always crystal clear, and everything was ok with life when I came down.

A Peruvian sound healer once started his session by asking us what we most loved to do when we were four or five or six years old. I didn't hesitate: climb trees, dance, play jokes on people, write letters, make music. Then he asked us how often we did those things as adults. Along with almost everyone in the group, the answer at that time was, "Very little." He'd become a sound healer in his forties when he remembered that as a little boy, he was always playing his flute, making music. It was what he naturally did, naturally gravitated to.

Our souls guide us early on to show us what makes us happy, maybe even what we're here to do.

What did you love to do when you were little?

"If You Don't Know Where You Come From, You Can't Know Where You're Going."

— ANDREAS STILB

Do you believe in magic?

Five years ago, I embarked on an ancestor tour in Europe, curious and compelled to see who and what I could find in the countries of my known ancestors—Germany, Poland, and Lithuania. I had always identified as being Polish and Lithuanian, despite growing up working in the German restaurant of my relatives. I felt connected to this lineage, maybe because these were the ancestors about whom the stories were told. I felt Polish and Lithuanian, not German.

Armed with a few scraps of information and the verbal lore of my Polish and Lithuanian immigrant grandparents, along with a thick book of German genealogy charts dating to the 1600s a cousin had traced, I bought a one-way ticket to Europe to find what could be found.

Despite the few Lithuanian and Polish breadcrumbs I had to follow, the villages and relatives of my ancestors appeared with an almost magical ease. Seemingly impossible synchronicity followed synchronicity, as though I were being led by some unseen force.

But despite my pages of German genealogy, I was barely able to locate the small village in the Palatinate Forest from which my German ancestors emigrated. When my husband and I searched the graveyard in this town for family names and looked online for local relatives, we came up blank. I didn't have a particular fire in my belly to find these ancestors, didn't feel connected to them, and was inexplicably uncomfortable as we walked every inch of the town.

Ready to leave, I stopped in the village church, knowing that ancestral threads are often found in the records. As my eyes adjusted to the dark, I was immediately drawn to a wall of pictures of the war dead and found myself looking straight into the eyes of four young men—boys really—in Nazi uniforms and bearing the names of my ancestors. I reeled backward and felt like I'd been punched in the gut. I felt like throwing up.

My father was a U.S. WWII combat Marine, all my uncles had been in the war, some Lithuanian relatives had had their land stolen and their family members machine-gunned in their own home, and my Polish relatives lived in the thick of the fighting and the camps. No wonder I now had a war of my own going on inside of me. The DNA of all these ancestral factions—German, Polish, Lithuanian— were swirling through my body still fighting it out, now battling in me.

My brain couldn't wrap itself around the fact that I was related to these young boys in Nazi uniforms. Of course, the war dead in Germany would have been wearing Nazi uniforms. Who knew if these boys were Nazi sympathizers themselves or had just been drafted as collateral damage in a war that they and their families abhorred? I wasn't ready to find out more. And I wondered if this was why our family identified as Polish and Lithuanian, brushing the German ancestry under the rug. Don't talk about it, and it doesn't exist.

Except it does.

I'd seen enough and was ready to move east toward Poland. But seeing the names on the wall reminded me that my ancestors came from here. I remembered that I was actually there to pay homage to my long-ago ancestors, without whom I wouldn't exist today.

I wrote a note in the church visitor book: "I'm here to honor my ancestors, Valentine Stilb, Phillip Stilb, Anna Neuss, Johannes Stilb, Gertraude Keilhaus, Catherine Mang, etc. Thank you for making new life. Your great-great-great-great-great-great-great-granddaughter Diane Pienta, Boston, MA, July 2017."

I promptly forgot about the note and was physically, emotionally, and mentally relieved that there were no living relatives to meet who might have a swastika hidden in their living room.

No, I did not want to be German. Except I am.

Four and a half years later, I found myself, in an almost impossible coincidence, in the very room my mother died in on the first anniversary of her death. I had just spent the past year wandering without a home base, without a clear sense of purpose or work, a little lost and rootless, like a tree that had been dug up but whose replanting spot—if it would ever be planted again—had not yet been decided. On this night, after having searched in vain for so long for just the right home, on just the right piece of land, amid just the right strong community of like-minded souls, I felt as deeply directionless as I'd ever been in my life.

In a moment of rather bizarre instinct, I decided to check my Facebook messages, something I do reluctantly about every six months. A message blinked brightly at me: "Is this the Diane Pienta who wrote in the church records in Heltersberg in 2017? I'm the last remaining relative—please contact me! Please come visit your homeland as soon as possible. I have all the stories and history of our family."

It was signed Andreas Stilb. Cautiously at first, then with joyful connection, I virtually met this warm, funny, authentic, positive, good-hearted man, a relative of my generation who shares a deep love for the land and ancestry. A person who has opened his home to Ukrainian refugees; is a positive contributing influence in his community, and who is now in my life. A man whose daughter improbably has the same name as my sister's daughter. The tagline on his email signature? "If you don't know where you're from, you can't know where you're going." I asked if he always used this tagline. No, he'd never used it before. It was something his grandfather said, and without knowing any of my story, he felt compelled to include it to me.

I returned to Boston the next week and immediately saw a bus with the billboard "Next Stop . . . Germany." I'd never seen this bus before, but now it kept pulling out in front of me. It advertised the Goethe Institute in Boston, which, established in 1967, had been designed to "promote an ongoing dialogue and exchange between American and German artists and experts to help shape a current understanding of Germany today." I had denied, resisted this part of my past, of where I was from, out of fear of what I'd find. Until the candle was lit in the darkness, I couldn't see the beauty, strength, connection. Couldn't see the magic.

Those boys in Nazi uniforms?

In another almost-impossible twist of fate, this book is in the last day of the final edit, about to go to the publisher, and I'm writing this paragraph in

Heltersberg, Germany, staying as a guest in the home of the Stilbs, who it turns out, are some of the most positive, joyful people I've met; people I'm proud to be related to. It's as though the ancestors are wanting to write this ending.

We spent hours walking the village in an ancestral history tour, led by Andreas. We heard about how difficult the war years were—how Andreas' mother and her family hid in the forest under rocks to avoid the bombs. How there was little to eat and only the heat from the cookstove in the winter. The church just happened to be open as we walked by, and as we entered, my gut clenched with an eerie sense of déjà vu as I wondered how to approach the pictures and ask if these boys had been Nazi sympathizers. As though reading my mind, Andreas explained that the four boys all came from one family. Their father had been arrested and put in prison for some time, accused of plotting against the Nazis. The boys were pawns—cannon fodder—in the atrocity of war, not collaborators. There were five boys in this family, one too young, but the four eldest were forced into service to a war that was not theirs, and killed.

My perspective shifted from distrust to deep compassion in a second, as I sent them and their family love.

Making peace with all parts of ourselves can have some far-reaching, unimaginable effects. Is there something in your past you don't like to look at? Maybe an outer circumstance or an inner fear? Is something calling you to look at where you've come from, literally or figuratively?

Do you have relatives you can't believe you're related to? Ancestors you'd rather not acknowledge? What if you learned their stories? Sent them love and healing? What if they're waiting for you to acknowledge them?

To know and accept where I come from, both in this life and in my ancestors', makes peace. I feel like all the warring factions and nationalities in my bones can put down their weapons and sit down together at a delicious peace feast.

Maybe, just maybe, if enough of us do this, we can create peace in the land.

Is there some part of you waiting for you to make peace with her?

Even The Smallest Actions Have The Power To Transcend The Biggest Wrinkles. Do Not Discount The Small Ritual Practices Toward The Light.

This phrase came to me in a very dark period when I just couldn't see light at the end of the tunnel. The combination of physical illness, loss, grief, and a floundering in the world made me throw up my hands and say, "What am I even doing all these spiritual practices for—yoga, meditation, energy healings, journaling, and on and on? They clearly aren't helping me. Maybe they're even hurting me!"

The very next sentence in my journal is the one above. I understood: just as practicing scales on the piano every day for weeks can feel like nothing is happening or a waste of good time, one day, seemingly out the blue, we're playing the arpeggio that eluded us. Magic happens.

And so it is with our ritual practices toward the light. Everything is easy when days are good and time is plentiful. But being as devoted to our practices as we would be to a soulmate or a lover, even when times are tricky or we're bored or lazy—therein lies the power.

Just make sure you love your practice to begin with. There are no shoulds here. Find your joyful practice, then do it. There's power there for you.

What's one small action you can take each day, maybe for the week? Here are some ideas:

- Write three things you love about yourself.

- Meditate for eight minutes.

- Visit your favorite tree or plant for ten minutes.

- Watch the birds for five or ten minutes.

- Write three things you're grateful for.

- Watch funny video clips.

- Spend five minutes reading something that inspires you.

No step toward the light goes unrecognized by the light.

Perspective

"When head is grounded
Sky becomes ground
Canyons grow out of Sky
A new perspective.
It's not what you think it is."

—DIANE PIENTA

Do you ever look at things upside down?*

I mean, literally, do you ever hang your head and look between your legs, so it looks like the sky is what you're standing on and the ground is above you? When you were little, did you lie in the grass with your feet pointing up so you were walking on the sky?

I went through a period of looking at things upside down a lot. I'd hang my head down or kneel while putting my head on the ground, even attempting a headstand to see what the world and people looked like inverted. It was one of those periods that had people around me asking, "What weird stuff is Diane up to now?" Do not let these kinds of comments or people deter you. They are often the most repressed.

By putting our hearts above our heads, we can view situations, people, or the world through our heart instead of through the filter of our minds, which often generates the same, old, less-than-joyful reactions and words. I just thought it was fun. It made me giggle for no reason, which I hadn't done in a very long time, and I found myself being lighthearted.

We so often want people or situations to change, to behave differently so we ourselves can feel good, to have them see our point of view, to see how we view the situation. But what if we turn the situation on its head— literally—to get a different perspective? Turning a multifaceted crystal in the sunlight can suddenly have it refract into a rainbow. We are multifaceted beings, so what if by shifting our perspective, we can have the illumination of a rainbow?

After my father died, my mother spiraled into advanced Alzheimer's, living alone in her home of sixty-five years while vehemently resisting any moves or help. She called the police in a rage almost daily, believing that the neighbor next door was breaking in to steal cans of soup and her bra. My sister and I were at our wits' end.

As is so often the case in these situations, sibling rivalries and resentments surfaced that we both believed had been long forgotten. Maybe in all partnerships, one or both people sometimes feel they're shouldering more of the burden, doing more of the work, and this was definitely coming up for us.

There was one particularly painful, hour-long phone call. We were going round and round, trying not to accuse, blame, or guilt the other, digging ourselves in further and further, each trying to get the other to see her point of view. We were getting more entrenched and not getting anywhere, when I suddenly remembered: go upside down.

I got on my knees and planted the top of my head into the carpet. This made it nearly impossible to speak, so I just held the phone to my ear and listened. After a bit, there was no charge to what my sister was saying. Her words were no longer filtered through my lens of "I'm carrying an unfair load of this burden." It was just . . . interesting.

When she stopped, I heard words come out of my mouth. I swear I don't know who spoke them: "When this is all done, it's just going to be you and me, and I want to have a loving relationship with you and your family." What? Who said that?! It was a hell of an end-run around my protective ego. And with no effort on my part except to move my body. Just a different perspective. A perspective from the heart. A spiritual perspective. It shifted everything.

What if you looked at something upside down? What if it's not what you think it is?

And now—a public service announcement. Hanging upside-down is not risk free. If you've never done this before or if you haven't in a long time, if you have certain medical or musculoskeletal issues for which this move may be contraindicated, or if you're even remotely uneasy about giving it a go, let caution be your guide and look for an alternative. One good option is to lie on your back with a pillow under your spine to elevate your heart and put your feet up, maybe resting them on the wall.

"The Magic Is Everywhere, and an Open Heart Can Always Tap into It."

—GABRIELE FLORES

These were her parting words to me as I left Gabriele Flores's beyond-enchanting, magical retreat at La Duna.

La Duna Centro Ecológico is a remote sanctuary outside La Paz, Baja California, where the desert, mountains, and Sea of Cortez come together. Golden light plays off red canyon walls, the dark night sky is ablaze with starlight, and you can hear your heartbeat in the silence. Simple, lovingly prepared organic food is served three times a day, and sleeping casitas are open to the pure air. The more-than-human world reigns in this place, with the desert flowers, birds, lizards, and butterflies, the dolphins and the whales. Creativity here seems effortless, as though nature herself were using humans to generate ever more beauty. At La Duna, it's easy to feel as though you're being held in the arms of the Divine.

Wise woman Gabriela Flores is owner and creator of the center. I had just finished thanking Gabriele profusely for creating and tending such a magical place and for sharing it with me and others. I loathed to leave this cocoon to drive into vibrant, loud, dusty La Paz for the next leg of the journey, and I expressed this, too.

Gabriele didn't miss a beat. "The magic is everywhere," she said, "and an open heart can always tap into it."

Forest therapy guides will sometimes broach this idea, too. Is our love of nature unconditional or conditional? Do we love nature only when she is pristine, gorgeous, untouched, exquisitely groomed? Or can we love her equally when she is strewn with garbage or trampled or paved? Can we really find the magic everywhere we go?

I've been playing with this as we recently moved back into the city. This move was not made out of desire; it was a necessity. I'd been hankering to live immersed in pristine, gorgeous nature, and here I was in the midst of vibrant, loud, endless-construction-noise, lots-of-garbage city nature.

So, where's the magic?

Well, when my heart is open, the magic is in the huge flock of birds chirping wildly in the carefully manicured shrubs in front of the building.

It's in the wisdom of the century-old trees around this neighborhood who have seen so much and who hold strong and steady and graceful through it all, showing me how I, too, can be beautiful and steady even in the midst of adversity.

It's in the exploration of the nearby Muddy River, who has been paved over and contorted into pipes and conduits and yet still gorgeously attracts the herons and endangered frogs and ducks even as the diesel trucks and sirens roar by.

It's in my new yoga community that has welcomed me with open arms.

It's in my research of this land, in my discovering that in the 1600s, this was an area of rich salt-water estuaries and marshes. A sacred, magical place where the rivers met the bay, a beautiful fertile place for fishing and farming, for life. Though completely filled in and paved over now for "progress," that sacred land is still under my feet as I pound the pavement to the nearby yoga studio, groovy bookstore, and organic food store, which is another version of magic that serves my modern-day needs and desires.

Suddenly, the magic is everywhere.

If my heart is closed, this is all invisible to me.

If my heart is open, I can see the magic.

If I can see the magic, I can honor the magic.

And by honoring the magic, I can be the magic. Everywhere.

What magic is around you right now?

On Adaptability

I've been watching this wily creature named Covid for a while now—two years and counting. I've feared her, despised her, been annoyed and frustrated by her, inconvenienced by her, and have shaken my fists in anger at her as she raged around the hospital as my mother lay dying.

She's like an annoying relative who's stayed long past her welcome. And yet I've started to get curious about her. Yes, she's destructive and chaos making, but she's also, if nothing else, adaptable.

In ancient times, the best warriors wanted to fight other strong opponents; it was considered dishonorable to joust with someone whose skill was inferior to your own. And strong opponents, it turned out, were also the better teachers.

What can I learn from this Covid creature? "Adaptability," she whispers. "Shapeshifting," she hisses. She is not just flexible. She is adaptable. As the vaccines take hold, as one form seems to be under control, she morphs into a new form—nimble and quick and clever. Quietly. She doesn't need fanfare. She simply looks at the situation and adapts to her new circumstances. Done.

There is an elegance to this kind of shapeshifting. Some might call it evil or insidious, and it can be those things too. But some of the most powerful teachings come from the darkest moments, if we dare to look a little closer, to become curious about the strengths of our opponents and ask what they can teach us.

Sheesh, if we could do this, how much easier would life be? No— how much more interesting and fun would life be? If instead of complaining or worrying about the roadblocks thrown in our path, what if we put on our cloaks of adaptability and morphed—the same person, but a different form? You might say we are doing this anyway, out of necessity, and this may be true. But what if we could view it as an opportunity to be super creative and playful in how we adapt? This feels powerful.

Do you have a challenge that you're really annoyed with? Where you want someone or something else to change?

How can you shapeshift to maintain your power in a new form?

> *"The secret of change is to focus your energy not on fighting the old, but on building the new."*

—SOCRATES

"The World Is Full of Lonely People Waiting for Someone Else To Make The First Move."

—PETER FARRELLY

We just never know who's lonely, do we?

Sometimes it's obvious, the person who is so clearly alone and hungry for connection. But often, that person who seemingly "has it all together" is often the loneliest as they fill their hours with achievements and busyness.

Yes, loneliness is part of the human experience, and we'd do well to become our own best friend so we don't depend on others to fill us. And yet belonging and connection are two primal human needs. It's estimated that lonely people are fifty percent more likely to die prematurely than those with strong social connections. Harvard Medical School just published a study that shows isolation in lab animals causes the kind of brain shrinkage and changes seen in Alzheimer's.

The Amish weren't kidding when they determined that the worst punishment they could inflict on someone was to shun them.

Do you love when someone reaches out to include you? To check on you? Yes, me too!

When I moved to Boston in my mid-twenties, I found myself, well, a little lonely. Having grown up in the Wyoming Valley of Pennsylvania, which is also called the Valley with a Heart, I wasn't prepared for the Yankee reserve in New England, which can border on caution, even wariness or downright unfriendliness at times. Being self-employed and knowing no one made it a little hard to break in, even as I joined musical and gardening groups.

I was "putting myself out there," extending myself to make connections and making the first move. But in the early days, it was sometimes lonely.

I met Ann a few years into my move. Unwittingly, some of that Boston-cool had seeped into my bones as I watched her energetically bound across the street to where I gardened in our new front yard. I probably would have just waved at her across the street and said a friendly hello. "Hi! I'm Ann! I love your garden!" she bubbled and launched into a story about her own garden. We talked animatedly for about an hour, learning that we both loved cooking and gardening and how her husband shared a passion for wine with my husband as we excitedly planned to have a meal together.

On the surface, I'm sure I didn't *look* lonely. I was busy with work and music, gardening and renovating. We were engaged with family members. She would have had no idea that I was a little lonely for a pal.

She made such a great first move, and the four of us became fast playmates.

Do you beat the greet, or do you wait for someone else to make the first move? As Plato, Philo, or Ian MacLaren may have said, "Be kind, for everyone you meet is fighting a battle."

Maybe we can create a more beautiful world by being the person who makes the first move. Is there someone today you can share your beautiful self with and make a connection?

On Wonder

"Sell your cleverness. Buy bewilderment."

—JALAL AL-DIN RUMI

Sometimes, in moments of insecurity, I catch myself trying to be clever. You know, speaking in a way that suggests a confidence I don't feel or speaking with a kind of authority to sound smart, or, well, clever.

In her book *The Infinite View*, Ellen Tadd teaches that insecurity is antidoted by humility, not with cleverness or the attempt to impress, which just seem to make the situation more awkward. Humility may seem counter-intuitive, but it's what allows me to know that I'm just one part of the grand whole, and knowing this in my bones opens the door to. . . .

Bewilderment! Wonder! Curiosity! This opens up a whole new world. A world of lightness, of freedom and play. It's said that play is the highest form of learning, and curiosity is an entry point into play. Curiosity is engaging. It means we're secure with not knowing.

Do you find that "not knowing" isn't exactly highly valued in our culture? We want to be the one with the answers, the expert, the one who knows and is looked up to as the authority. Beginner's mind has somehow fallen out of fashion.

I'm no tarot reader, but I do know that in the tarot, the Fool is often portrayed as a beggar or a vagabond, with ragged clothes and no shoes. But the Fool also represents new beginnings, inexperience, not knowing what to expect, while being comfortable, even excited, with this state. The Fool is often considered one of the most powerful cards in the deck.

Are you an expert or a beginner? Or both? What if you turn your expertise into curiosity for a day? What if today, you live life as a beginner?

"Always be on the lookout for the presence of wonder."

—E. B. WHITE

The Queen of Trust Is Nature Herself.
She'll Teach You To Trust Yourself If You'll Let Her.

A couple of years ago, I was visiting ancient stone circles in the English countryside. The leader of our group gave a brief explanation of one particular site, how it was used ritually, seasonally, and for healing by ancient people, how these sites had powerful energy lines running through them deep within the earth, how our ancient ancestors who still had their animal nature naturally knew about this force and how to work with it. This was a sacred power site, and to top it off, wild horses now roamed among this group of stone circles.

The setting was enchanting, and a few of us walked slowly into the circle.

Almost immediately, I was overcome with emotion, which seemed to last for a very long time. I was knocked to my knees, weak and weeping—an intense, powerful experience that I still don't understand and that honestly kind of scared me. This place was magnificent. There was majesty and magic to it, and yet my modern brain couldn't quite wrap itself around the idea that the energy of this circle could have that kind of effect.

Despite my keen interest in energy and ancient sites, and despite being an intuitive, a part of my modern, educated brain still questioned whether these sites really had that kind of power. Maybe I just ate something upsetting for breakfast?

I've found that this is a theme in my life, and I watch it in others. Our animal nature, our gut instinct, will tell us one thing, sometimes speaking very softly. But our modern, highly sophisticated brain will jump in loudly with "That's ridiculous!" and discount it if we can't figure it out, if there's not a scientific study that proves it, or if it tends toward the magical.

I don't know about you, but I'm almost always sorry when I don't follow my gut and am never sorry when I do.

After what seemed like hours but was only thirty minutes, I collected myself and walked out of the circle, stopping to turn and look back. I watched as the pack of wild horses galloped together, straight toward the edge of the circle. When they reached the outer rim of the stones, they all stopped abruptly as though on cue, standing stock still for about a minute looking into the circle. They waited in perfect stillness until the lead horse stomped his right hoof on the ground, and as though receiving a signal, the horses all walked slowly, stately, grandly through the circle, only running wild again after they passed through on the other side.

What do you make of this?

Watching the wild world interact with itself creates a truth and a trust we can't deny. My brain tried to make me doubt my own experience. And yet when I watched the horses interact with the circle, I didn't think, "Oh, those horses are faking it. They're just putting on a show. These must be those woo-woo horses who believe in energy lines." Their animal nature was so vital. So powerful. So authentically attuned to the world and to themselves. I understood then just how divorced I am from my own animal nature that's been tamed out of me, out of all of us, in the name of progress.

What if we trusted our own powerful inner knowing as easily and gracefully as those horses? What would it be like to go through life with that kind of awakened sixth-sense extrasensory perception?

You don't need an ancient stone circle and wild horses in England to learn from nature. She's right outside your window, even if you live in a city. Sitting still for just fifteen minutes in nature will calm your mind like the best of meditations, and watching the birds or the ants can connect you to your inner knowing in a powerful way.

Is your animal nature trying to tell you something? What does it whisper to you?

"Never Rationalize Anything That Feels Wrong."
—LOUISE HAY

Sitting in my office doing work I disliked on a gorgeous, bright spring day felt wrong. But I rationalized that I simply had to do it. You know, responsibility to clients, bills to pay, all that. Did I? Really? Would the world have stopped turning? Would I have been fired if I took the afternoon off and soaked up the sunny spring sun and air? Or would I have been filled with the incredible beauty of nature and been more productive? Or maybe if I did it enough, I would have quit that job and been led to something that filled me as much as did the magnolias and lilacs buds bursting forth and the birds singing loudly to each other.

I knew someone who called herself my good friend but was emotionally abusive. I rationalized that we need to accept everyone where they are, that I didn't want to hurt anyone's feelings, and that I didn't have all that many friends in this new town, so I couldn't afford to alienate her. But I felt that her behavior and our relationship were just wrong.

My husband said that he was going to invite his father and his father's wife to purchase the land next to us. This felt dead wrong. But I rationalized that I was a bad person for even thinking this. This was his father, for goodness sake! I rationalized that as a new, young wife, I didn't have the authority to say what I was intuitively feeling, that it seemed fraught to be that close.

Rationalizing what feels wrong means we care more about making nice or not rocking the boat more than we care about how we feel. It can mean we value other people more than we value ourselves. More than trusting and honoring what we know to be true.

We've been conditioned in this modern world to trust our brains rather than our hearts or our intuition. And here's the thing about rationalizing something that feels wrong: it never works out. We can try to blame it on someone else or on a bad situation, but the fact is, we're upset because we're the ones who went along with it.

The job I had? It took me getting cancer to quit after rationalizing it for years. The "good friend?" She was emotionally abusive for weeks shortly after my mother died, chastising me for not being upbeat enough, before I put an end to that relationship. The in-laws next door? Well, that's a classic story you yourself could probably write the end to—good neither for us, nor I suspect, for them.

Often the stakes are not so high. We can rationalize little transgressions more easily. But anything that doesn't align with our integrity slowly nibbles away at our soul.

Rationalization can come at us from the back door, too. I was short and shirty with the post office clerk who told me she needed identification, which I didn't have, to open a post office box. The rules seemed insane. I was exasperated with her and wasn't very nice. I didn't feel good after the exchange, and I'm pretty sure she didn't, either. I started rationalizing that she should have been helpful to me, but my spirit didn't let me get away with this. It felt wrong. I had no reason to be unkind, regardless of the circumstances.

Are you rationalizing anything that feels wrong to you? What if you simply stopped and said, "This doesn't feel right." What if you gave it a voice?

I bet your soul would kiss you.

"Bitterness Keeps You from Flying."

—LORI MCKENNA

In Victoria Benoit's book *Three Magical Words for a Magical Life*, she quotes Dr. Rick Hindmarsh: "I have been a physician for four decades and have seen more lives destroyed by bitterness than cancer, addiction, heart disease, and contagious diseases combined."

Ah, bitterness. The original word comes from "to bite" or "pungent taste." Like if we chewed a lemon peel and it left a bitter taste on our tongue or if someone does something hurtful and "leaves a bad taste in our mouth."

How to get rid of a bitter taste? Well, if it's in our tastebuds, we can cleanse our mouth—floss, brush, rinse with mouthwash, and put something good tasting in. It might take a little while, but eventually we have a fresh, clean palate.

If it's in our hearts, then what? Isn't it the same thing? We can flush out our hearts with forgiveness, swirl mercy through our cells to rinse them out. We can pour in something we love to help bitterness move on, creating a lovely, delicious, expansive taste again.

If we were experiencing a bitter taste from eating, say, lemon peels, most of us wouldn't just keep talking about how we had a bitter taste while reaching for another lemon peel. So why do we sometimes do this with our hearts and minds?

Why do we sometimes feed bitterness, retelling the story of how we've been hurt or wronged by another? Sometimes for years? Or a lifetime? Why do we keep reaching for the lemon peel instead of rinsing it out for good?

This word, *forgiveness*, is such a powerhouse, no? And do you find it can sometimes be so hard to do? Mahatma Gandhi wasn't kidding when he said, "The weak can never forgive. Forgiveness is the attribute of the strong." Though as some other wise person quipped, "Forgiveness doesn't excuse their behavior. Forgiveness prevents their behavior from destroying your heart."

I heard the line about how bitterness keeps you from flying in the song "Humble and Kind" shortly after an experience with a long-time friend. We'll call her Susan. My mother had died in the midst of our move out of a home and community we had lived in for thirty years. She was the last of her generation, and it seemed that I had lost both my childhood homeland and my grown-up hometown at the same time. To top it off, my husband was just re-diagnosed with cancer. Oh, and there was a worldwide pandemic. I was in a grief-and-healing mode, unexpectedly sad at times and wanting to be immersed in softness, nature, and love. We embarked on a previously planned boat trip with Susan and her husband, after explaining that the death of my mother, combined with the departure from our community and Dave's diagnosis, was hitting me unexpectedly hard. That I was having a rough emotional time and was prone to grief.

Not once asking how I was doing or if I was ok, she instead chastised me for not being upbeat enough, for being sad, for bringing the mood down, telling me she was interested in Fun! Adventure! Juicy conversations! Not sad faces and inconsistent moods. Being trapped on a boat with her was beyond painful. And to top it off, as she and her husband departed our boat, not once thanking me for the nightly meals I cooked for them, barely acknowledging my presence without saying goodbye, she shimmied up to my husband, gushing over him as she told him how extraordinary she thought he was. It was gross. I couldn't stand her.

When I returned home, I was thinking of the creative projects I wanted to get off the ground. How I wanted to fly with them. And then I heard this song. It told me that my bitterness would keep me from flying. Damn! I did not want to forgive her. She was a mean you-know-what.

But *I* wanted to fly.

So I started looking. What was that experience all about?

Well, it made me admit that I was angry with myself for allowing her to stay on the boat as long as she did. It was clear within days that the situation was not good. For any of us. And yet I didn't say what I needed, which was for them to leave.

I also had to admit that I had never really trusted her in the first place with my heart. We had never spent more than a few hours together, in the twelve years we knew each other. In my heart, I knew spending weeks together was a mistake. But I didn't want to be the party-pooper, despite needing to be around supportive, loving people. So again, I acquiesced to be nice and to "go along with the crowd." Which wasn't good for them, either.

And the million-dollar question was, why had I allowed someone like that into my inner circle for so many years in the first place?!

As only Oprah could put it, "True forgiveness is when you can say 'Thank you for that experience.'"

It would have been really nice to not have needed an experience like that to propel me to say what I need and want, to listen to my own heart and to honor it instead of going along with the crowd. But that experience was the crash course I needed to put my foot down and say what I need. I know I won't put myself in a situation like that again. And for all that, I'm grateful. I'm now able to see the gift in the experience, to start to be thankful for the encounter. And in that thank you, there's forgiveness, there's fresh, crisp air, new breath. I can feel wings sprouting on my back with the wind rising beneath them.

Is there some bitterness in your heart that could use a rinse-out? Please, I want you to fly.

Focus on The Love, Not The Wound

The other day I caught myself anticipating a negative reaction from an acquaintance before we even met. I just "knew how she was," and I started running a negative scenario in my mind that I thought was likely to unfold. I *knew* she'd say something thoughtless or negative. So then I rehearsed what I'd say to her, or, insidiously, how I'd maintain a calm, spiritual perspective in the midst of her negativity. Why was I manifesting this future that didn't exist?

Do any of you do this, or do I have the monopoly on this kind of crazy?

Maybe you've escaped this trap, though I see a lot of others enacting this same weird drama. So then I can breathe, laugh at myself, and remember Tal Ben Shahar's words, "permission to be human!"

But really. Why do we focus on the wound, past or anticipated, when what we want is love? Peace? Fun?

You can read hundreds, maybe thousands, of books on neuroscience to dig into this question, to understand how we groove the patterns of our brains to expect a threat and how the more we think this way, the deeper the groove, so that we roll in a wicked kind of cycle. We can read and understand, but in the end, we're the ones who actually need to do something to change our groove.

Friends, can we develop ourselves into new kinds of humans? Maybe the kind who regularly expects love? Anticipates delight? Looks for awe?

Given the choice, do you feel better running a negative scenario in your mind or remembering a crazy-fun, laughing-out-loud day with people you love? Would you rather feel fearful or interested? Would you rather feel anxious or at ease? Angry or playful? So here's the thing: you do have that choice.

Focusing on the wound doesn't feel good. Sure, it might give us a rush of self-righteous adrenaline in the moment, and it's that high we keep chasing, running it over and over in our minds and deepening the groove. In the long term, though, it puts us in prison.

When you start going down the rabbit hole, can you catch yourself and refocus on something beautiful, generous, creative? Something or someone that excites you?

It can be hard!

And you can do it!

Be nice to yourself if it doesn't happen all at once. It took you decades to groove that record. Sandblasting it smooth will take a little time.

Listen for and expect miracles.

The World of Comparison Is Never a Good Place To Be

Look at the Apple tree! She does not say, "Oh poor me, I wish I could be like the elegant evergreen Pine tree who stays glossy and green all year long." And the Pine tree, he does not say, "Oh my, I wish I could be like that lovely twisted Apple tree covered in red orbs of juicy fruit loved by animals and humans alike."

But we humans! We do this comparison thing, looking around to see what others are doing, creating, having—how they are being—as a way to inform what we might do or have. Being inspired is one thing. Wishing for another's beauty just invites sadness.

So what to do? How about loving up our own beauty and gifts? Are we even actively aware of what amazing talents and gifts we have?

How about you jot in the margins here ten things that are magnificent about you—what the world gets to enjoy by you just being you. Can you embody that grace and know in the same way that the Holly tree wears her pointy, green glossy leaves, and brilliant red berries. Genuinely owning her brilliance, neither flaunting nor hiding it?

What a delicious way to live, friends. Is there any other?

Transition Time

How do you Transition between your daily activities?

It was the end of a yoga class, and I was feeling really good. I'd been practicing for about fifteen years and had the confidence that can come with competence. I felt like my poses were strong, open, and fluid.

So when the teacher closed the class with, "Watch how you're transitioning from one pose to another; the space between the poses is more important than the pose itself and is the true yoga," I did not like this.

What transition?! What spaces?!

I couldn't remember one moment of transitioning in the entire ninety minutes of what I had thought until then was a damn good practice.

How we do anything is how we do everything, so I started looking for where else this was showing up in my life. Turns out, it was everywhere.

Usually, I was so busy rushing to get to the next pose or life activity that I wasn't even aware of the transition. Did I think the transition was unimportant, while the pose or the activity was important? Well, yes, I did. Could this be why I always felt rushed? Like there was never enough time? Why my transition from life to yoga class often included me scrambling, driving fast, hellbent on getting to class, where I could then be calm and Zen? Life is sometimes too weird.

When my to-do list is a mile long, I usually run from one activity/ phone call/appointment to another. It's in our culture, this "time-sickness." Dr. Larry Dossey coined this term *time sickness* to "define the belief that time is slipping away, that there's never enough of it and we've got to go faster and faster to keep up."

So I started creating "transition time"; five or ten-minute spaces between the activities during which I just sit, be quiet, and do nothing except . . . transition. The first time, my husband saw me sitting on the sofa in the middle of the day doing *nothing*. "What are you doing?" he asked. "Don't interrupt me, please. I'm having transition time." He's used to these sorts of things by now.

At first, five minutes of silent transition time was hard. When time feels short, when I'm running behind, when there's more to do than can get done in a day, the idea of sitting in empty space for five minutes between activities can seem downright irresponsible—unproductive, lazy, and even more stressful.

There are a million ways to transition.

But here's the crazy thing. Quantum physicists tell us that time is malleable, fluid. I really don't know how this happens, but when I slow down, time slows down, and suddenly there's more than enough time for everything. Life flows. Creative ideas and impulses can come out of nowhere in that space, too.

One day I made myself sit for "just five minutes." I was nearly crawling out of my skin because there was so much to do, but I told myself the transition time was equally as important as the activities, and being a perfectionist, I wanted to get good at transitions.

As my mind slowly calmed down, my eye lit upon an unread book on dowsing. Something told me to pick it up, and an hour later, I was entranced. Clearly, what was so important could wait! That moment led to studying for a month in England with a master dowser and seeded a deep love affair with the English countryside. In other words, magic was planted in the transition zone.

The empty space, the void, is where creation begins. If you're an artist, you might be accustomed to looking at the world this way. The empty space between plants is what gives form to the landscape design, or between objects in a painting. Forest therapy guides might refer to this space as the liminal zone, where we're not fully immersed in our wild-animal mind nor our modern-thinking mind, but an in-between place of not knowing what will come that is often the space of the greatest growth and development.

I started seeking and finding the liminal space everywhere. My fingers exist because of the empty space between them; otherwise, they'd be a mitten.

How do you transition? Out of bed? Into bed? From work to home? From one appointment to another? Is there empty space? Is it calm, unhurried, observant? Is it frenetic, rushed, unaware?

How do you want it to be? Can you play with it?

What's The Worst That Can Happen?

When I'm considering a leap out of my comfort zone, when something is both calling to me and pushing my big buttons of discomfort, I'll play the What's the Worst That Can Happen game. The rules are pretty self-explanatory.

Take a sheet of paper and write down "What's the worst likely thing that can happen if I do this? Will I die or get badly hurt? Will I lose everything I own, everyone I love?" My answer to this has never been yes.

Then ask, "What's the worst likely thing that can happen if I *don't* do this?" Here's the answer I usually get: "The worst that can happen is that you'll always wonder if you should have done that thing, and if you don't do it, you'll be depressed, not playful, not joyful or singing or dancing or laughing or making beauty, and then you'll die." *That* is the worst that can happen.

I employed this game when, on a whim, I arranged to go to England for a month to study earth energies and dowsing with a master dowser. I'd read her books, wasn't interested in online classes, and contacted her to see if she would teach me privately in her hometown in England. We had a brief chat and scheduled time in February.

After I found a charming cottage to rent, made my flight arrangements, and was coincidentally gifted a set of dowsing rods, I thought, "WHAT AM I DOING?" I hadn't had any prior experience dowsing or reading energy lines. I was showing up in one of the coldest, darkest, wettest months in a small town in the countryside where I knew no one. I had no idea if I could even sense the energies, or if I'd like it, or if I'd click with the teacher, but nonetheless had contrived to employ this well-known rock-star dowser to be my private instructor. This was starting to feel pretty uncomfortable and more than a little crazy. I thought of all the other things I *should* be doing that month instead—getting my résumé and website up, a million other things. It was so much money. Surely there were better uses for that money?

There are plenty of scientific studies that show how the brain just does not like change and can send us quickly into protective mode. Getting out of our comfort zone is big-time change, and sometimes, we have to coddle the brain, coax it along so that we feel safe, so we can get excited instead of worrisome about all the things that could go wrong.

I played the game. What's the worst likely thing that could happen if I went? I wouldn't like it, and I'd end the escapade and catch an early flight home. Oh.

The magic that happened that month in England could fill another book. Excitement can often feel like fear, but our spirit soars when we stretch out of our comfort zone. In fact, it's often our spirit who's leading us there; we just need to get out of the way, trust, and say, "Yes!"

Is there something you're called to do that's pushing your comfort zone buttons? What's the worst that could happen if you did it?

"Twenty years from now you'll be more disappointed
by the things you didn't do than by the ones you did.
So throw off the bowlines. Sail away from the safe harbor.
Catch the trade winds in your sails. Explore. Dream. Discover."

—H. JACKSON BROWN JR.

Knowing Our Own Worth Is More Valuable Than All The Gold in The World

Do you know deep in your bones how preciously worthy you are? How does it feel, knowing this? Have you thought about it?

Can you think of a time when you've been unconditionally loved by someone special in your life? Or maybe it was a time in nature? One of the ways we feel unconditionally loved is by feeling safe, accepted for ourselves exactly as we are. Knowing we aren't being judged or needing to prove anything. Knowing we're deeply worthy and deserving, not because of anything we've done or not done, but simply because we are here.

Knowing and trusting my worth in a humble yet powerful way allows me to stand compellingly steadfast in myself when the winds of disharmony, conflict, and disagreement rage all around me. When I don't know or trust my worth, I get sucked into the dramas of others and the world.

Knowing my worth is what gives me confidence to put my creative work out in the world without fear of rejection or disappointment. I do it to serve myself and my spirit, not for the approval of others.

Knowing my value has me trust, deep in my bones, that I belong on this beautiful planet—and so do you. That we are each, every single one of us, a contribution in our own extraordinarily magical way.

Knowing my worth brings a contented inner peace, a gentle happiness and powerful energy.

But how do we do this? How, we might ask, do we create this deep trust and knowing? As Joy Stone observes, "You are your own constant companion in this world." So we may do well to befriend and love this companion who isn't going anywhere anytime soon.

Here's one approach. What if you wrote down, right now, what you really admire and like about yourself? What are you good at? What are your talents? What qualities do you love about yourself? What are your special gifts? What's your secret superpower?

Try doing this every day for a week straight and see what happens.

Sharing our extraordinary gifts in the world is a good next step. Confidence comes with action and service; it makes our hearts happy and our souls sing. Is there more of you and your gifts that you can share with the world now? Even a little bit more?

How can you immerse every cell and bone in your body with the deep, contented appreciation of your incredible, gorgeous, life-giving worth? I'll take worthiness over gold any day of the week.

"Love yourself first and everything else falls in line.
You really have to love yourself to get anything done in this world."

—LUCILLE BALL

"When You're Stuck in Dance or in Life, Take a Walk."

—TONI BERGINS

What do you do when you're stuck?

Toni Bergins was leading us in one of her power-boosting, soul-soothing Journey Dances. As we tuned into the music and her guidance, melding with our own rhythm, I was totally in the groove, in flow. And then I wasn't. Trying to get back in sync with the experience just seemed to make it more difficult.

Toni, ever tuned in, stopped dancing, turned, and started swiftly walking around the room. "When you're stuck, take a walk. Everybody, take a walk," she said. "In dance, in life, or whenever you're stuck, just take a walk." So I did, and then, suddenly, I was in the groove again.

Does this sound too simplistic to you? Are you saying, 'well, of course'! But how many times do we just sit in place and spin our heads, trying to "figure it out," trying harder and harder as solutions become more and more elusive?

Spiritual traditions across the ages guide us to turn away from our problems. We can take this to mean mentally turn away, but we can physically turn, too.

A few years ago, I was explaining to my non-spiritual, non-yogi, non-meditator, non-anything-remotely-woo brother-in-law, Tom, about a wonderful meditation practice I was doing to create expansion and unstuckness, to create new brain patterns; a somewhat complex combination of breathing, visualization, and energy flow.

He listened patiently. Then, wrinkling his forehead and looking confused, he asked, "Why don't you just go for a walk in the woods with the dog if you want to clear your head?"

Gosh, I could have saved myself years of study. He's right, though. This works too—although the best of us can keep the gears of our brains going full speed on a walk. Have you ever taken a long walk in the woods, totally in your head, and not remembered a single tree or bird or stone? Where your feet were in the forest, but your head was somewhere else? But even the action of taking a walk, moving our bodies, especially in nature, can shift our perspectives.

Forest therapy can show us a way to be in nature in a way that connects and attunes us with our ourselves and the world of creation, where new ideas, thoughts, and solutions emerge, although this is not the primary aim of the experience itself. There are plenty of studies for the science-oriented among us that show how being outdoors in nature positively affects our brain chemistry and blood pressure, creating powerful, specialized natural-killer cancer-fighting cells, shifting our thinking, reducing stress, helping us focus better, helping us be kinder and more creative, and improving short-term memory. She really is a magic panacea.

For instance, just now, feeling a little grumpy as I try to find (with continued frustration) a compelling scientific study to illuminate my point, I think it's time to practice what one preaches. Unhunching from the desk, I stretch and walk out to the garden, where I greet my neighbor, Lynn, bury my nose in a sassy, full-blooming peony named "Sorbet" for just a few minutes, and am now back with renewed perspective. Who needs to hear about yet another scientific study? There are about a thousand you can find with a click of Google. Or you can just move your body, go outdoors, and see for yourself.

Amy Cuddy made "power poses" (now called postural feedback) all the rage a few years ago with her TED talk, showing how we hold our body affects our moods and actually changes our body chemistry, influencing how confident or powerful we feel. By moving our bodies in different ways, we create different outcomes, think different thoughts, and say new and unexpected things, including coming up with new, creative solutions and perspectives.

What if you stood up right now and walked around the room, or better yet, went outdoors? What if you swung your arms wide and then raised your hands over your head as you walk, then waved them back and forth overhead? What if you walk really *sllooowwwlly*? What if you walk briskly and sprightly? Then what if you shouted "Yay!" over and over for no reason as you walked? Come on, what do you have to lose?

Our Life Force Is a Function of Participation.

The other night, a dark cold New England night, when the sun set at 4:30 p.m. and 6 p.m. felt like midnight, I was dreading the neighborhood association meeting I had agreed to attend. I didn't want to sit on yet another Zoom call with people I didn't know (I was new to the neighborhood) talking about what I assumed would be tedious, mundane issues debated ad nauseum. I had just broken my ankle and figured that that was as good an excuse as any to absolve my attendance and go to bed early.

And then my eye happened to alight on this quote: "Our life force is a function of our participation." Sigh. "Ok, I'll sign on for fifteen minutes, introduce myself, and make an early getaway, so at least I can say I participated."

Ninety minutes later, I was loathe to sign off as I listened to a group of smart, caring, community-oriented folks discussing all kinds of changes and projects happening in my neighborhood that I hadn't even known about. I was energized! Excited! Interested! This is so often what happens when we just show up and participate. Magic can happen. More to the point, we have no idea what magic might be created just by our showing up.

How often are we just too tired, too busy, not interested enough to be a "Yes!" to life? Even things that we might want to do—an art class, a singing group, a winter picnic? How often do we think, "Oh, it's just too much trouble this week?" Or if we do attend, how often is it done halfheartedly?

What if, for one week, you said "Yes!" to whatever opportunities came your way? Just one week, even when you feel like saying "No!"— cheerfully, joyfully saying "Yes!" to whatever people and opportunities cross your path. That would be some experiment, no? I wonder what you'd find.

Participation is the soul and essence of what it means to be human.

More on Adaptability

Have you ever found yourself in a place or situation you didn't want to be? Where, by dint of choice or circumstance, you looked around and asked, "How did *this* happen?"

Dave and I landed with a thump back in Boston after six months of camper-van living, chasing Shangri La. Our quest to find a delicious morsel of land and home to create sanctuary, magic, and community had proven elusive. As winter set in and a medical diagnosis appeared, our synchronicity now led back to one of the loudest and busiest locations in the city. It was rough. Sirens wailed, turnpike traffic whizzed, and cars gunned it 24/7. Nature girl was not happy to be back.

I bought the best earplugs I could find. Often walked to the grocery store with my head down and hands over my ears. Told myself I was the one who finds beauty and magic wherever I go. Told myself inner peace is available anywhere—it's inside of *me*. But friends, it was jarringly loud and assaulting, and I felt like I was bullshitting myself. I was not happy.

Busc, my fellow empath and magic-making friend, came over one afternoon. As we talked in the living room, our conversation abruptly screeched to a halt as four sirens pierced our ears at the same time, horns honked, and a helicopter whapped above us. I looked at him and said, "I don't know if I can deal with this."

"Girl, you gotta adapt," he said. "Yeah, I know," I mumbled. "I gotta be flexible." "No! You need to ADAPT. Adaptability is not flexibility. It's changing shape. You gotta *adapt* to your surroundings. You gotta change *your* shape to fit this environment, this situation."

He left, and I thought about this. How so many of our immigrant ancestors came to this country and adapted to live in circumstances that wouldn't be their first choice or maybe even their last, and they went on to thrive. How the people who adapt are the most resilient, while the ones who resist their circumstances so often fall into hopelessness. How so much of our energy is often used in resistance to circumstances or people we don't want to deal with instead of shifting ourselves to meet the situation.

The *Oxford Dictionary* definition of adaptability is "the capacity to be modified for a new use or purpose." I clearly had some new as-of-yet unknown purpose. If I wanted to find out what this was, I was going to have to put on my shapeshifting cloak, snap my fingers, and alter my state.

Turns out my new purpose was to learn to be the eye of the storm, no matter what was going on around me. Sure, I could be Zen with the best of them in an idyllic setting or the meditation station, but the universe was now asking me to walk my talk in the midst of frenzy and a raging storm. A friend coined this "being a light and love warrior in training." I accepted the challenge.

I decided I would shapeshift into a true urban dweller. To see what I could learn, I talked to people who *loved* the busyness of the city. I delighted in the yoga studio that was so busy it had multiple classes on the hour. I walked to museums and libraries, made sure I did what I loved as much as possible to be in creative flow where time and sound don't exist. I sat on benches and watched the never-ending parade of diversity in the people who walked by—old-timers elegantly attired, pink and purple-haired college students in jack boots, girls in short mini-skirts and bare legs on a thirty-five-degree winter day, academics debating systems theory, and homeless guys asking for a buck or five. I listened to dozens of foreign languages being spoken on the street. Walked everywhere, discovering all the nooks and crannies and secret spots that reveal themselves to those on foot who look. Traced the Muddy River history and watershed from her mossy banks to where she flowed into the bay. Got involved with the local neighborhood association and community center. Even bought hip urban clothes and thick, black-rimmed eyeglasses to more fully play the part. Soaked up all the goodness, creativity, and vibrancy the city had to offer, knowing that nothing lasts forever, pledging to look back at this time and see not resistance but delight.

It's so easy when we look at someone else's life, no? We can easily see what's so great about it and wonder why they might be focusing on what's wrong. But sometimes, it's not so easy in the mirror.

How about you? Is there something in your life you're resisting? Can you think of one small way your beautiful being might adapt?

We Don't Laugh Alone, and We Don't Love Alone. Or, On How To Be a Good Friend

Not long ago, I broke my ankle. Dave was out of the country, and I was living in a third-floor walk-up. We had just moved back to a new part of the city after being away for over a year, and I didn't yet know my neighbors. Even as the pain screamed otherwise, I was in denial that I had done more than sprain it. "Surely I'd be fine in twenty-four or forty-eight hours," I thought as I crawled around the apartment on my butt, breathless from the pain and shock and wondering how I'd get food.

I texted Bunny, a friend I hadn't been in touch with for nearly a year and who lived across town. "Do you have an extra pair of crutches?" the text read. My phone rang immediately. "What happened?" Bunny demanded. "Oh, I'm sure it's nothing. I fell on some leaves. I just need a pair of crutches for a day or so until I can walk on it again."

Bunny didn't miss a beat. "You need to go to the hospital." The prospect of negotiating the ER by myself in the middle of a pandemic while I was in shock was just too daunting. "No, I'm sure it's fine, I just need some crutches." Again, not missing a beat was Bunny: "I'll be at your house in an hour. How am I going to get in?"

I felt an incredible surge of relief wash over me. Bunny spent that afternoon and evening with me, getting me fed, running to the store for pain relief, and trying to convince me to go to the hospital. As she literally tucked me into bed, she said, "I'll be back at 6:30 tomorrow morning; the ER will be empty, and you can get it checked out." At 6:30 a.m., she was back at my house to take me to the ER. She waited for me to be examined and then insisted I come to her home, where she fed me turkey bone broth and amused me with stories in between naps on her sofa when she went to fill my prescription and called our mutual girlfriends, who immediately asked what they could do.

At this point, I felt I had taken up way too much of her time. I knew she was busy with family, work, and the upcoming holidays and that I should ask her to get me home even though it felt so good to be cared for like this. As though she'd read my mind, she urged me to spend the night.

I was overcome with so much gratitude for her care, her love, her friendship. I asked myself, the one with the never-ending to-do list, "Would I rearrange my life over a thirty-six-hour period and care for a friend I hadn't seen in a year, with this level of love, compassion, and care?"

As Bunny wholeheartedly invited me to come and stay at her home as long as I needed or wanted, tears came to my eyes, and thanks rushed to my lips.

Looking me straight in the eye and speaking straight from her heart, Bunny passionately exclaimed, "It is very important to me that you don't feel alone in this. I absolutely don't want you to feel alone while you're dealing with this. We don't laugh alone and we don't love alone. We are meant to be there for each other."

Amen.

To feel another's vulnerability and to interrupt our own busy lives to make sure another doesn't feel alone in their pain—if this isn't God's handiwork I don't know what is. The ripple effects of this can shift the world.

I ask myself, "Who would I interrupt my life for?" Best friends and family, yes of course, but acquaintances, strangers?

Our community is one of the most accurate predictors of our health, happiness, and well-being. Who do you laugh with? Who do you love with? With eight billion people on the planet, there's a tribe, a community, waiting for you if you haven't already found them. If you have, you are blessed beyond measure. If you are looking, just ask and see who comes your way.

I don't want you to feel alone.

Geese fly seventy percent further and faster when they fly with others than when they fly alone.

Shhh. All in Good Time. No Need To Force Anything. Enjoy All of IT. Time for Calm.

What do you do to quickly shift yourself from anxiety to calm? With anxiety at an all-time high around the globe, it seems this might be a good skill to have in our back pocket.

Have you considered the sound *shhh*?

In the Vimala alphabet writing system, the ligature *sh* represents divine timing and being divinely guided to our true purpose or profession. It's the sound of knowing that everything's happening in perfect time and perfect order. It's the sound we make to soothe a crying child. Or ourselves. *Shhh*. Hush.

Try saying it out loud—don't be shy!—and see if you experience a sense of calm wash over you.

When I find myself overwhelmed or really pushing myself to get things done, I'll take a moment and whisper *Shhhhh*, just as if I saw a child in distress (but not like an ornery librarian).

I invite you to take three deep breaths and read this next part really slowly, softly, out loud, and see what happens:

Shhhhh, it's okay.

Shhhhhh, time to get quiet.

Shhhh, Shhhhh.

Shhhh, it's okay.

Shhhh, Shhhhh.

Almost anywhere in the world, if you want to quiet someone, you say *Shhh*. Some traditions teach that *shh* means silence or stillness, and in qigong or other Eastern healing modalities, the sound *shhhh* is used to help heal and support the liver and small intestines, which in our modern world are almost always stressed out.

It's free, it's quick, it's painless. Why not try it right now for sixty seconds and see how you feel?

Focus on What You Do Want, Not on What You Don't Want.

"Of course," I thought, as an astrologer proffered this advice. "You're giving a lot of time and energy focusing on what you don't want," she continued, "instead of what you *do* want." Really?

Having always considered myself a very positive, upbeat person, looking for the bright side of life, as they say, I was stunned to learn that what was actually coming out of my mouth was how I didn't want to be working so many hours, how I didn't want our house to continue being a construction site, how I didn't want to deal with my challenging mother, and on and on.

But what did I actually want? What do you want?

We don't want pain or suffering, don't want discord among our friends and family, don't want misfortune. But what do we actually want?

The late master healer Dr. Pankaj Naram estimates that nearly ninety-five percent of us don't actually know what we want, and he sees this as the biggest cause of disease and distress. We hear all the time how our thoughts create our reality, how negative thoughts lead to more negative thoughts. Uplifting thoughts lead to other uplifting thoughts, actions, and realities.

What do you want?

What's coming out of your mouth?

What do you want—really, truly, in your heart?

What would make your heart absolutely sing and your soul soar?

What would make you want to jump out of bed every morning to greet the day?

I wonder what you'd write if you asked your heart this question, picked up a pen, and filled a page with the answers.

Patience Is Not Passive. Subtle Is Not Weak.

Herbal teacher Linda Patterson of the Boston School of Herbal Studies noted my look of dismissal when she described one particular herb's actions as "subtle." As a beginner, I was interested in knowing who the powerhouses were. "Don't ever confuse subtle with weak," she advised. "Some of the most subtle herbs are the most powerful, and while you're at it, make sure you don't confuse patience with being passive." Some of the best advice to date.

It seems we've "evolved" to prize Action! Big Action! The Bigger, the Better Action! The loudest voice wins! When did quiet, patient, and subtle evolve to suggest weakness, ineffectiveness, or being uninfluential?

One definition of *subtle* is "delicately complex and understated." One source traces its etymology to meanings that evoke being "penetrating, ingenious, refined, sophisticated, intricate, adept, wise, well crafted, precise, accurate, or of keen judgement." Gosh, I would like to be subtle.

Although I'm aware, I can still find myself falling into stereotyping—like, the person sitting back and observing the situation patiently isn't a "leader," or the quiet person is not enthusiastic. In her book *Quiet*, Susan Cain illustrates so beautifully how we as a culture undervalue introverts and that we lose so much by doing so.

We are all so action-oriented—self included!—and I'm learning more and more that true potency, inspired action and speech, most often come from taking a patient pause and letting the action come from the stillness.

Are there places in your life where you see patience or subtlety as weak, when in fact, it might be your greatest friend? Where can you insert some subtlety? Is there something you can be patient with?

"Shouting at a Flower Bud Does Not Make It Open Sooner."

—CHRISTINA FELDMAN

Growing up, I was shouted at. It was the 1970s, and enlightened child-rearing was still in its infancy. It didn't make me stronger, faster, smarter, happier, or nicer. It didn't make me like or respect or want to agree with the people who shouted at me. It made me feel like a rosebud looks when there's an unexpected frost and the edges get all burned and turn brown and its head droops, when it's unclear if the tender little bud will actually open at all now or just sag more and drop off the stem, unopened.

Friends, don't shout at people, or yourself. Don't be mean. Don't cut them down. No matter what they're doing that you don't like. No matter how much you disagree with their politics. You hold tremendous power in your voice, in what you say and how you say it, in the energy and intent *behind* what you say.

When I visit my garden, I exclaim enthusiastically to my plant friends, "Wow, you are so beautiful! Holy cow! Look at how much you've grown. Look at all your buds. You're magnificent! I love having you in the garden! Man, I am so happy to see you." I swear their heads stand a little taller, a little prouder, and their colors radiate a little brighter.

Do you say things like this to yourself? Or do you say things like, "Crap, I can't believe I was so stupid yesterday." What would you like to hear?

You can use your voice to create something beautiful in the world or use it for destruction. You choose.

You can create the most gorgeous rosebushes, dripping with the most magnificent roses bursting into a perfumed, cascading bouquet, or you can create scorched earth. Do you create flowering meadows of exquisite wildflowers? Or do you create parched, barren patches?

You hold tremendous power in your voice. Who are you?

"People will only remember how you made them feel."

—CARL BUEHNER

Ask for a Word

When you're in the thick of a flummoxing situation, or even when you've just got *questions*, do you ever wish you could call for a takeout order of wisdom to be delivered?

There's a game I like to play, compliments of clairvoyant counselor and teacher Ellen Tadd, called Ask for a Word. To clarify, we're asking here for an "enlightened" word. Sometimes, when I'm not sure what to do or feeling off, I'll ask for a word of the day, to learn from, and let it teach me. Don't try to think of a word that you *think* would be good for you. In fact, try not to think at all. Let the word come to you, to pop into your consciousness. You might be surprised at what comes.

When I took some time off from my twenty-five-plus-year business career, I worked on a local farm. My boss was newly promoted twenty-four-year-old Barbara, who had clearly not gotten the memo that top-down management was now passé. She barked orders at us, pushed us to work harder and faster, and tried to stop any conversations. Humor was sorely missed, and it seemed that a mutiny might be in order. I had more experience with customer service, plants, gardening, and business in my left hand than she had in her whole being. People had always said this was a super fun farm to work at, but it was seeming a bit dour.

She was really pushing my buttons. Has something like this ever happened to you?

After being reprimanded one morning for not watering the plants fast enough, I decided I could either quit or ask for a word. I asked for a word.

What came in was *tolerance*. Really? "Ok, tolerance, this better be good. What can you teach me? What do I need to know here?"

What flooded in was a long-forgotten memory of me at twenty-four. I had been promoted, possibly prematurely, to manage one of the largest departments at a Four Seasons hotel, with five assistant managers, fifty employees, and staffing needed from 6 a.m. to 1 a.m. I was proud to be selected—and completely in over my head. The stress was incredible. I was working so many hours just to keep my head above water. And suddenly, I saw, so was Barbara.

At twenty-four, I hadn't had enough life experience to not take that job so *seriously*, to do the best I could but to not have it give me ulcers, which I was letting it do. And suddenly, I saw that Barbara was practically giving herself a heart attack trying to meet an impossible schedule.

I remembered cynical, old-timer employees who had more experience in *their* left hand than I had in *my* whole being as I tried to figure out how to interact with them, inspire them to attend to customers quicker, and keep service areas cleaner. Often insecurely aware of my youth, I remembered employees who cheerfully agreed with my requests and those who fought me, those who wanted me to succeed, and those who wanted me to fail.

I remembered the breeziness and freedom of the hourly employees who clocked in for their shifts but ultimately held no overall responsibility for the operation and how heavy the weight of responsibility felt on my shoulders. Now, I was the breezy, free, clock-in for a shift/don't take any stress home employee.

One definition of tolerance is the capacity to endure continued subjection to something without an adverse reaction.

How could I be in this situation without having an adverse reaction? How could I maybe even have a positive reaction?

I decided right then and there that I would be one of the people who wanted Barbara to succeed, cheerfully agreeing to requests and whatever was presented. While I loved not having responsibility for the operation, I approached my shift as though I had ultimate responsibility for the work. That I would be tolerant, with no adverse reaction. I didn't really enjoy her personality any more than I had before my thought shift. But I liked myself and the situation a whole lot better.

It changed everything. Now, this really was a very fun place to work.

Words have energy, and by focusing on uplifting or enlightened words, they can have a powerfully positive affect on us and those around us.

This morning, feeling agita without knowing why, I asked for a word. My old friend *tolerance* showed up again. This time, it was to be tolerant with myself, to not push myself so hard to get everything done, to be tolerant of myself when I mess up. The energy of tolerance eased the edges, lightened things up, softened the harshness.

It changed everything.

Below is a list of enlightened words from the book *The Marriage of Spirit: Enlightened Living in Today's World*. This is only a partial list, of course, there are many others. As author Leslie Temple-Thurston explains, these are heart-centered states of being. She describes them as "cleared, or, balanced emotional states." If you feel them rather than just read them, you may get a sense of balance, stability, or peace.

Maybe you'd like to read over them and ask what word wants to play with you today.

Have Fun!

Appreciation	Attunement	Awe	Balance
Beauty	Bliss	Clarity	Compassion
Connection	Detachment	Devotion	Discernment
Enthusiasm	Equality	Equanimity	Eternality
Faith	Flow	Forgiveness	Generosity
Grace	Gratitude	Harmony	Hope
Hospitality	Humility	Imagination	Impeccability
Joy	Kindness	Loyalty	Neutrality

continued next page

Openness	Patience	Peace	Play
Silence	Serenity	Tolerance	Trust
Unconditional Love	Unity	Wisdom	Wonder

Become a Vociferous Blesser.
Bless Everything in Your Path. Watch Magic Happen.

This morning, I got up and was just kind of in a *mood*. I had hoped to get up early and write but slept in and felt like I was trying to catch up to myself at seven o'clock in the morning. This did not bode well for the day ahead. I reminded myself, "I can change this." There are so many practices that can help shift our negative mindsets. Gratitude is one of them. Friends, do you find it hard to be grateful when you're already in the middle of a downward spiral? I do. Even after practicing these kinds of things a long time.

My list of "I'm grateful for this clean water to brush my teeth, for my friends and family, x, y, z" felt forced and empty.

But then, I started speaking *to* everything I touched and saw them as though they were old friends, which of course, they are. You could say I started blessing everything. "Hello, beautiful blue bathroom sink, you old friend! Thank you so much for helping me to keep my teeth and face and hands so clean and delivering the perfect temperature water at the flick of a faucet! You're amazing!"

"Hello, my hands with your beautiful opposable thumbs, all you fingers in perfect working order allowing me to brush my hair and write with a feather pen and make celery juice for breakfast, oh my gosh, it's endless what you do—you are so incredible—what would I do without you?!"

"Hello, toilet. You know, you probably have no idea how happy I am that you take away all the smelly crap and waste right out of my house with one little push of a lever. I'd have to go outside to an outhouse if it weren't for you! Thank you so much!"

Suddenly, I was connected, in relationship to *everything*. I started feeling kind of giddy. David Abram writes about the concept of the world watching us—that we are not the only ones observing (or not observing, depending upon our mindfulness) the world around us. This invites us to playfully picture that the world and everything in it observes . . . *us*. Do I want to be observed as an ornery, frustrated, middle-aged woman? Or as someone who is vibrantly alive, joyful, and in love with life?

How do you want to be seen?

Gratitude lists can sometimes feel, well, like a list. We shift our mindsets into positivity much more quickly when we can *feel* the thankfulness or *feel* the connection. Have some fun and try it. Speak *to* and thank those faithful friends who serve you each day—your kitchen table you've spent hours at, your loyal computer, your phone that is like a body-part appendage—whatever is true for you. See if they don't possess an aliveness that makes you delighted to be in their company and in the world herself. Watch what magic happens.

Let Your Life be a Prayer.

Become a Good Receiver, as Good at Receiving as at Giving

Are you a good receiver?

When someone compliments you, do you beam and say, "Thank you so much!"? Or do you wave it off saying, "Oh no, that's not true!" or "It's nothing," or even "No, no—thank *you*"?

How about when someone gives you a lavish gift? Do you feel you need to reciprocate, or can you just bask in the love and generosity that someone else wants to bestow on *you*?

What about when someone who is not as well-off as you gives you a very generous gift, when you know they had to stretch in some way to give you this gift?

Does it make you uncomfortable? Do you ever attempt to give it back? Tell them you don't need it?

And my favorite—how do you respond when someone gives you something you don't want, don't need, or really don't like?

Thank you is such a powerhouse word and opens us up to so much abundance.

My late mother-in-law was a prodigious gift-giver, generous beyond generous. She loved to shop, both for herself and for other people. And she loved to give gifts. Gift-giving was one of her ways of showing love. Lucky for me, she had beautiful taste.

When Dave and I were newly married, she constantly showered us with items from her home. When she moved, she encouraged us to take plants from her magnificent, award-worthy garden. She never arrived at our house without some wonderful gift, often from her travels— beautiful linens, a marvelous necklace, funny salt-shakers, a handmade leather piece. And when she downsized, we received furniture, rugs, art.

In my late twenties, starting off with very little money, I was so thankful, delighted, appreciative. It was like having an insta-house delivered out of nowhere.

But in my early forties, after spending two exhausting years clearing out my parents' stuff-laden home of sixty-five years from which they threw *nothing* out, including the receipt for the orange, vinyl La-Z-Boy recliner purchased in 1972, I was on a mission to purge.

I looked around our large house and mostly saw . . . stuff. Without children, I wondered, what were we doing with all of this stuff, and who was going to deal with our own stuff when we got older? I was most happy living outside in my tent with the trees and the birds and did so often in our urban backyard. I wasn't a collector of things.

As she continued to generously give us gifts, my attitude shifted from appreciation to "Ugh. More *stuff*!" One afternoon at her house, she and her husband pulled out two large silver candelabras they'd received for a wedding present forty years earlier. They were large, ornate pieces. As my husband eagerly said, "Yes! We'd love them!" my knee-jerk response was, "Ugh! No more stuff!" Cringe-worthy words.

I would have done anything to reel the words back into my mouth the second they left my lips. For them, it was a generous gift of something special. A gesture of love. Had I been operating at my best self, I would have thanked her profusely and later asked her help as we were attempting to downsize ourselves.

Great gift-giving is an art. To find the perfect thing for someone means you've taken the time first to know who they really are and what would make their heart happy, then find or make that very thing. You take yourself out of the equation and see the world through their eyes, and this, really, is the ultimate gift.

Great receiving is also high art. Can we always see the gift in what's given, regardless of whether we actually like it?

Some say being a good receiver requires self-love. To accept a compliment with easy grace means we believe we're deserving of such praise. The same thing with a lavish gift. Can we accept that someone is showing us their love without feeling that we owe them or that there's a scorecard?

Whether I may not like, want, or need something doesn't mean someone else wouldn't love it. I now love getting gifts that I don't want, need, or like. I love asking friends if they'd like this object I've received, and I love the look of delight on their face when they say yes! It keeps the flow going.

How do you receive?

I Always Have Enough To Be Generous

I was reading about a woman in India the other day. She was very poor, maybe even homeless. But she wanted to help the poor orphanage school she passed every day. She wanted to be of service.

She wasn't educated, so she couldn't teach, but she found many half-used pencils and erasers thrown out near the wealthier schools. So she made it a point to go through the trash every day to collect these pencils and erasers that still had so much life and creativity in them. She delivered them to the orphanage school, which sorely needed them. Her donations had such a big impact that she started going through all the trash in the wealthier schools, and she expanded her reach to other areas of the city, with an eye for anything and everything that could be reused. She made daily deliveries to "her children."

Wow.

To have that kind of generosity of spirit is breathtaking. Life-giving. Expansive. This practice—"I always have enough to be generous"—is so easy when we're feeling flush and secure. But how about when we're in survival mode? When we're stressed? Or when we're not getting what we want or think we deserve?

Martín Prechtel teaches that the quality of our life is not determined by the hand we've been dealt but how well we play that hand, not in terms of acquiring more, but how well we live in service to something grander than ourselves, generously feeding life herself and leaving the world better for a time beyond our own.

If a poor, uneducated, possibly homeless woman in India can make such a positive impact on others, what can I do with the incredible hand I've been dealt? What can you do?

I sometimes wonder, if I write a check but that check doesn't make an impact on my quality of life, is that really being generous? Is my spirit being generous? If I write a check but then don't spend even a few minutes to ask the homeless guy I walk by every single day what his name is, what his story is, and generously give him the dignity of human contact, am I really generous? These are questions, friends. I don't have the answers. What do you think?

The spirit of generosity is such a noble way of being. Generosity helps others feel seen and heard, loved, and appreciated. What a fantastic energy to generate and spread in this world of ours. What if every single person on the planet was generous just once a day? Holy cow.

I can generously give time, even when I'm in a flurry, to have a conversation with someone who needs an ear.

I can generously allow others their opinions when I unequivocally don't agree with them. When someone behaves badly, I can generously give the benefit of the doubt that they might be having a hard time and not assign a negative motive to their words or actions.

I can eagerly and generously praise this magnificent world early and often, thanking the sun and the stars and the trees and the embarrassingly overflowing riches of nature.

I can generously share with others all the wisdom I've been taught over the years.

I can generously find what's beautiful in others and acknowledge their gifts as often as possible.

I can generously remember to bring corn to feed the birds every morning on my walk in the park.

Oh, and I can even be generous with myself, showing myself kindness when I mess up.

What can you be generous with?

I always have more than enough of everything to be generous. How 'bout you?

Acknowledge At Least One Person Each Day

How do you feel when someone truly acknowledges you? Does it ever bring you down? No, me neither! I'm uplifted; the moment is somehow brighter, lighter, and the feeling can linger, sometimes through the day. It's no wonder Mark Twain said, "I could live two months on a good compliment."

Dr. Vimala Rodgers, who teaches Change Your Handwriting, Change Your Life, invited her students to send out a card a day (handwritten of course!) for forty days this past holiday season, the intention being to acknowledge people in our lives and invite them to welcome the new year with a happy heart. This seemed like a good idea. Why not?

Focusing on one person a day, expressing what I loved and appreciated about them, was the biggest gift . . . to *me*.

The words we use to acknowledge, to genuinely praise others, uplift us. Just by being present with these words and their bright energy puts us in a more positive frame of mind.

And as long-term intention researcher Lynne McTaggart tells us, focusing on what's great about people in our lives instead of what's wrong with them boosts both their and our spirits and health. Our thoughts alone are super powerful. When we add heartfelt words, it's like a beam of sunshine or a powerful vitamin.

Of course, they uplift the receiver, so it's a great twofer. But it's beyond a twofer. Being genuinely acknowledged (note, the word *genuine*—no phony, suck-up attempts here) makes it more likely we'll notice the good in someone else and pass that on. It's like the old Breck Shampoo commercial from the 1980s: the model liked it so much, she told two friends, and they told two friends, and so on, and so on (if you were born after 1980, you might have to Google this). But really—think of the impact you can have in your community by the ripple effects of just one acknowledgment!

I went through the usual suspects in a couple of weeks, so this exercise also had me reflect back on the entire year to see who else I could acknowledge.

The adage that some people come into your life for a reason, a season, or a lifetime resonated. I started to remember interactions with people that lasted sometimes just a day, a week, or a few weeks but at the time helped me in profound ways. And the list of people I was grateful for grew and grew and grew.

We never know the impact of our words. I remember working at a local farm, shooting the breeze as I trimmed geraniums in the greenhouse with thirty-year-old Sam one sultry afternoon. Sam talked about how he wanted to move to the West Coast, how he was so comfortable and happy there, how he really wanted to be a history teacher, how much he loved history, how his parents were putting the kibosh on this and wanted him to stay nearby in New England and get a "real job."

This otherwise quiet, nerdy, loner-type guy positively glowed with passion and came alive as he talked about various historical anecdotes. Like he was a different person. He animatedly relayed historical events through riveting storytelling, and I remember thinking, "Holy cow, this guy needs to be in front of a large audience, maybe be a college professor, who could incite love and interest in twenty-year-olds so we don't keep making the same mistakes over the next hundred years!".

I don't actually remember our conversation, but I'm pretty sure I just acknowledged his spirit, how his passion was so alive, so vibrant, so wonderful to be around when he was talking history! That he has so much to offer the world in this way. How he is an incredibly entertaining, gifted speaker and storyteller. That it seemed that his heart and soul clearly wanted him to pursue this dream, and it wouldn't get any easier the longer he waited, regardless of what his parents wanted. That he already had what it took to do it, and how I was inspired by his passion.

I forgot about the conversation seconds after it was over as I moved on to prune the marigolds. A year later, I got a message from Sam, thanking me for the conversation, saying that he was in Oregon and absolutely loving it, that he was getting a teaching certificate and wouldn't have done it without our conversation.

We just never know the impact of our words and what true acknowledgment can do for another, and maybe even ourselves.

What if this week, you acknowledge one person a day? I'd love to know what happens.

If IT Brings You True Joy,
Who Cares If IT's "Wrong"?
You're Here To Live IT All, Not Get IT Right.

Ok, before you get all up in arms, I'm not talking about doing something hurtful to others or the planet—nor am I advocating morally or ethically reprehensible acts.

What I'm talking about is "getting it right." Any perfectionists out there picking up what I'm putting down?

I was having a clairvoyant session with the inimitable, cheeky, sailor-swearing Judy, explaining that I really wanted some clarity about my life direction. I expounded on the fact that I was fifty (heavens forbid!) and didn't feel I had a lot of time to make "wrong" decisions. So a little divine clarity on what direction to take would be ever so helpful to keep me from going down the "wrong" path, with time running out and all.

But of course, it doesn't work like that. You know that. I know that. Yet still—how many of us look for the "right" path, the "right" partner, the "right" job, the "right" house, the "right" decision, sometimes staying in a pattern of indecision or inaction as we wait for a flash of clarity, as we beg for a sign? Signs that of course are constantly being handed to us as our fear of getting it "wrong" blinds us to their divine presence.

What Judy followed up with was, "Just find your F#*&ing joy and do it." She has a point.

What brings you joy? Do you do it? A lot? Like, everyday?

How expansive would it be to regain the freedom of a four-year-old who knows what they want to do and then does it. And when they're no longer having fun, stops. Does something else. This sounds simple, I know. So why does it seem so hard for us adults to do this? For so many, joy is just elusive. Maybe a burst here or there. But how many of us are really living our joy every single day? If you are, I honor you, and I'd love to meet for a cup of tea.

Why did it take me so long to claim myself as a writer? To claim myself as a felter? An intuitive and healer and fun-maker? To do what gives me true joy? I won't bore you with my ancestral patterns, though there are some hints in there.

Is this path I'm now on "right?" Feels that way most of the time. But mostly, I know I won't look back with regret and wonder why I didn't try writing a book, or why I didn't spend more time outdoors, or why I didn't share the teachings I've received from others.

Once something no longer brings joy, do you let it go easily or hang on to it for dear life? Or somewhere in-between?

To find our joy and "just do it," to make mistakes and course correct, to learn and laugh at the mistakes, to dust ourselves off, and to follow the next thread of joy—maybe that's what we're here to do. I don't think we've come here to suffer. Do you?

Our joy feeds joy in the world. It's energizing to be around joyful people. I think even the trees I visit are more uplifted when I'm joyful than when I'm complaining and suffering.

To be a joy bringer is a way of praising and thanking this beautiful world that we get to live in. Plus, it's just easier to sleep at night when we follow our joy than when we don't.

If you were here to "live it all," what would you do? What would you try?

How May I Serve?

The other day, someone mentioned that it would be wise to stock my pantry because economic forecasts suggested supply chains might go down this season. Not one to fall into prepper's fear, I brushed it off.

And then I started *thinking*.

Wait. What if supply chains really do go down? What would that look like? I'm in the middle of the city, not near farms. Maybe it wouldn't be a bad idea to stock the pantry? And would I want to be in the city if this happened? Where would I go? This could be really ugly. And so on. My vivid imagination was ready to spiral.

I recently discovered that one of the quickest ways out of a downward spiral is to ask this question to whomever or whatever you ask these kinds of question to:

"How may I be of service? How might I serve?"

Then listen to the answer and heed the call.

Lynne McTaggart, the renowned intention researcher, might call this "getting off yourself."

I've been asking this question daily. How can I be of service—to others, to the world? Then I watch and listen for ways to be of service. Sometimes it's small, like a kind word and a conversation with a homeless person. Lately, I've been getting, "Write your book already." Sometimes, it's listening to a friend who needs an ear.

Some of the most fun I've had is doing "guerilla good deeds"—anonymous good deeds that only the one who does them knows about. Like putting a little money in the pile of bananas at the grocery store for someone to find. Or cleaning up the sink in the public restroom so it's really nice for the next person. Or filling an expired parking meter. Or . . . what would you think was a fun deed?

Many of you are of service every day in the work you do in this world, often from within the walls of your home. I bow to you.

So back to stocking my pantry for the big meltdown. "Wait," I said. "How could I be of service if this really happens? Is it to take care of me and mine? Stock up and hunker down?" I had a flash of inspiration: What if I took my camper van and traveled wherever help and food might be needed in such a crisis? I visualized Di's Rolling Soup Pot. Of being part of a community that didn't stay home eating stockpiled ramen noodles but went out looking for ways to help.

Friends, I tell you, I shifted from fear to delight in less than thirty seconds.

As I write this, the situation around the world is generating even more heartbreak and fear. And at the same time, there are tremendous acts of inspiring service, compassion, help. We are wired to want to help, to be of service, in whatever ways speak to us.

I invite you to do one good deed every day for a month to see what happens. Tell us what magic bowls you over after you do this.

How do you like to be of service?

"Stay in Your Own Lane."

—DR. SUE MORTER

When I first started doing yoga years ago, I'd surreptitiously watch some of the other yogis and yoginis out of the corner of my eye, comparing myself to them, pleased if I was more flexible or balanced, annoyed if I wasn't. I'd catch myself and think, "Diane, you are such a jerk! It's yoga! It's not a competition. Mind your own business!" Or, "Oh, this is just too un-Zen to be comparing myself in a yoga class of all places!" But then I'd sneak another look. The ego is really something, no?

After a few years, slowly, slowly, my ego surrendered, and I was able to focus solely on my own practice, not even aware of anyone else's tree pose. *I was able to stay in my own lane*, and my practice was deeper, more satisfying, and more fun. And as is so often true with yoga, this seeped into my life off the mat. Life became peaceful, easy, and interesting.

A year into the pandemic, I started to flounder. *What* had I been doing the previous five years, and why wasn't I set up with an art studio, a coaching practice? Why wasn't I teaching or practicing all these healing modalities that I had been fortunate to study, leading meditations, or teaching wisdom? Why hadn't I written this book and others I'd been threatening to write for years? Why didn't I even have a website, for Goddess's sake? Where to even begin?

I found myself in comparison again. And this time, the results weren't so favorable to me. Others were stepping up to offer programs, to teach, to write. I felt as though I were playing catch-up. "Should have done this five years ago," my ego taunted. "Everyone else is so far ahead of me," I'd cogitate, even as I did my best to reframe this. "I am so behind the curve. I could have had a thriving business and practice by now. It may not even be relevant by the time I get up and running." And on and on.

"Stay in your own lane," said Dr. Sue. The image of a magnet inside my heart popped into my head, pulling my energy inside of me, of my body being a powerful vacuum cleaner sucking all of my straying thoughts and energy back inside of me. Of staying securely in my own car in my own lane, going the direction I had plugged into the GPS, not caring how fast anyone else was going or the direction they were headed. Not swerving left and right to see where others were going, what exit they were taking. Staying in my own lane and focusing on my own trip. Not only focusing on my own trip, *loving* this extraordinary trip I'm on! You can create an amazing trip. Right now.

Getting out of our lanes is dangerous. Wondering and worrying what other people think about our actions takes us into *their* lane. It creates fear and uncertainty on our path. We wouldn't drive into another car to ask, "What do you think about where I'm going? Do you approve? Do you like it? Where are you going? How fast are you going?" And yet we do this all the time with our life journey. I'm not suggesting that we don't collaborate with others or seek advice or expertise or even just share with a friend. But ultimately, we know the right path for us. And only we know it. Moving into someone else's lane only diverts and confuses us—not to mention possibly being deadly!

Staying in our own lanes doesn't just have to do with comparison. It's *anything* that takes us out of focus of what we love, who we are, and where we want to go.

That annoying conversation you keep running over and over in your head? Stay in your own lane. The worry about what's going to happen six months from now? Stay in your own lane. The regret over what happened ten years ago with people you loved? Stay in your own lane.

Where are you veering out of your lane? Come back. Get focused. Stay the course.

Stay in your own lane.

Hospitality Is Food for The Gods

Whose home do you love to go to? What about it makes you love it? Who loves to come to your home?

An ancient Slavic etymology of the word *hospitality* traces back to "lord of strangers."

So many of the old traditions teach that a guest in the house is God in the house. I remember an old Polish custom from Christmas Eve where an empty place was set at the table in case an unexpected visitor came to the door—the highest honor!

Being hospitable is one of the most noble ways of being in the world. To welcome in another and make them feel completely comfortable in your home, or in your presence, even when (especially when!) it's not convenient or you don't want to, is a way of seeing divinity and honoring it. Your spirit loves when you do this.

I remember stories from my first-generation parents of always giving the guests the best bed, even when there wasn't a guest room. The guest would never be given a pull-out sofa or a makeshift bed; the hosts of the house would sleep on those and make sure their guests got the best night sleep.

It's like the old Ovid *Metamorphoses* tale of Philemon and Baucis, who had lived out their long lives nobly but in poverty. Jupiter was about to destroy mankind and start over based on his experience with human greed and avarice, but he heard of Philemon and Baucis and decided to see for himself. Disguised as a weary traveler, Jupiter, joined by Mercury, passed through town knocking on the doors of the larger, more elegant homes for a place to spend the night, though no one invited them in. Coming to the end of the village, the gods approached the house of the old couple Philemon and Baucis, who, honored to have guests, eagerly welcomed them in, got the fire started with their remaining firewood, and made a meal with the precious little they had.

When they noticed that the pitcher of wine was always full no matter how much they poured from it, Philemon and Baucis realized that they were entertaining more than mere mortals, and they went to slaughter a goose, one of their most valuable possessions, though the gods intervened and granted them a divine wish for behaving with such noble hospitality, despite their poverty.

Maybe one way to exalt the divine and bring magic into our and others' lives is to practice radical hospitality, to become a lord of strangers.

It doesn't always mean welcoming someone into our home. It can be the generous act of a kind word or acknowledgment. Can we give hospitality to strangers on the street? To colleagues at work? To ourselves?

Is there somewhere you can extend your own magnificent hospitality today?

*"Hospitality means primarily
the creation of free space
where the stranger can enter
and become a friend instead of an enemy.
Hospitality is not to change people,
but to offer them space where change can take place.
It is not to bring men and women over to our side,
but to offer freedom not disturbed by dividing lines."*

—HENRI J. M. NOUWEN

The Guest House

This being human is a guest house.
Every morning a new arrival.

A joy, a depression, a meanness,
some momentary awareness comes
as an unexpected visitor.
Welcome and entertain them all!
Even if they're a crowd of sorrows,
who violently sweep your house
empty of its furniture,
still, treat each guest honorably.
He may be clearing you out
for some new delight.

The dark thought, the shame, the malice,
meet them at the door laughing,
and invite them in.

Be grateful for whoever comes,
because each has been sent
as a guide from beyond.

—JALAL AL-DIN RUMI, *Translation by Coleman Barks*

Don't Be Afraid To Walk in The Rain. There's Beauty There, and IT's Rarely as Cold as You Think.

It has been said, "Some people dance in the rain, others just get wet."

Weather bashing can be a sport in New England, where I've lived for thirty years. It usually goes something like, "Ugh, can you believe this [*fill in the blank—cold, snow, heat, rain*]." "I'm so done with this weather" is an oft-repeated refrain. The weather is often a "drag" or "ruining plans." Though some say it's a lucky couple who are blessed with rain on their wedding day.

Maybe you walk or hike or run or work in the rain, and so perhaps you recognize the aliveness that comes when we make friends with the elements—skin-hair-clothes wet, cheeks flushed. Wet and alive and connected to the water that actually gives us life. And maybe there's a newfound appreciation for our warm, dry homes when we peel off wet layers and rub down with a dry towel like a wet dog.

Maybe others see rainy days as indoor days, which can be fun too.

There's a meditation of sorts that can happen when you walk in the rain. I don't mean a put your head down under the umbrella, get this over as fast as possible walk in the rain. I mean a hold your head up to the sky, let the water drip all over you and feel it walk in the rain.

Like almost everything we resist, avoid, or fear, it's rarely as cold, uncomfortable, or scary as our minds will convince us it is. You might even, yes, love it.

Is there something you're resisting or avoiding? It might be fun to take a walk in the rain.

Slow and Steady Wins The Race

So then, why does it seem so many of us are running "behind the eight ball," as my dear departed mother would so often say? Even when we're not that busy? Why do we often have that underlying feeling of overwhelm that there's too much to do, or just that we're *so busy*?

My young, wise friend Tess calmly imparted this advice to me one day as we worked together at the local farm, where there is always way more to do than can be done in a day. I was working as fast as I could in the summer heat to water the parched plants, customers were asking questions and needed help, another large truck of plants was arriving to unload, and my heart was racing. Tess saw me turn swiftly to the truck. With her calm, gentle, lovely voice, Tess singsonged, "Slow and steady wins the race, Diane."

The next morning, my pen danced these words across the page . . .

> Slow it down to find the peace
> Panic has us going fast.
> Slow it down and make life last
> Slow it down to be strong
> Slow it down to stay on ground.
> Slow it down to win the race
> It's how much fun, not the pace.

Yes, I know. It's so much easier to say than to do. We're not used to slowing down in this culture. We're used to anxiety, which often has us going fast. But we get to either feed the panic with frenetic movement that produces more of it, or we can step outside of it. Slowing down our breathing is a good way of slowing down the situation, detaching from it.

Reading suggestions to "detach" from demanding situations used to annoy me. "If I could detach from it, don't you think I would have done that already?" I would sarcastically thought-bubble the author. I mean, sure, it's easy to detach when I'm in my favorite yoga studio all blissed out, but when I'm in the middle of juggling a million things and my heart is racing and the phone is ringing, then what?

Practice when it's easy so you remember in the frenzy. I like to practice in a long line in the supermarket, feeling pressed for time. Instead of checking my watch, I slow down and play with the time. I can't make others go faster, but when I slow down—I know this sounds crazy—the line moves faster. I ask the universe to open the way for me to be exactly on time for my next appointment while I take this opportunity to breathe, and honestly, friends, it nearly always works! I take it as an opportunity to practice meditative breathing—six seconds inbreath, six seconds outbreath. I usually don't even realize that I've arrived at the front of the line until someone behind me, who clearly has *not* been breathing six seconds in and six seconds out, barks, "It's your turn! The cashier is open!"

Talking to strangers in line can also do the trick. We can get to know ourselves by how we speak to strangers. How do we engage? Do we put our head down and ignore them? What do we say? What do we ask? Are we curious? Do we complain? It's hard to be stressed out when we're engaged in a fascinating conversation.

Traffic and stoplights and long lines are great places to practice holding ourselves slow and steady, all those places where we can't make the world go faster by our tension, but maybe we can hold ourselves slow and steady in the thick of it and in a twist of magic, help the whole world slow down.

Maybe we can actually have fun and inner peace as we run this race called life.

How do you hold yourself steady when the dust clouds of life are swirling around you?

*"Give Something in Nature Twelve Secret Names.
Do This Once a Week for The Rest of Your Life."*
—MARTIN SHAW

This challenge, issued by bard and mythologist Martin Shaw, sounded interesting, so I tried it—and was appalled at my seemingly defunct vocabulary and lack of capacity to come up with even a few luscious, honey-dripping-from-the-comb descriptions. It was harder than I imagined, and therein lies the key: imagine, imagination.

How easy or hard you find this exercise might be a good barometer of the health of your imagination. The health of our imagination determines, in part, the level of fun and play in our lives. And the amount of fun and play in our lives is correlated to the quality of our relationships with others, with ourselves and the world herself. You might say that giving our imaginations regular workouts can make us happier people.

To see and name the beauty of a birch tree twelve ways means I actually need to slow down enough to really see her. To see her in a way that makes me fall in love, at least a little bit. We tend to see all birch trees as "a birch tree." But every birch tree is as different as you and me. Quirky in our own ways.

What if we looked at our tree and spoke her beauty back to her so deliciously it made her blush? Gosh, what if someone did that to us? To have someone see our true beauty so clearly and reflect it back to us. Isn't this what we all long for in some way?

What if you tried it? What if you started by giving yourself twelve secret magical names? What's one right now?

"You can't depend on your eyes,
when your imagination is out of focus."

—MARK TWAIN

"I find, if I walk with a lilt in my step
Dancing and prancing with my right then my left
If I tip my hat with a bit of ridiculousness
I can cavort and frolic and be oh so so curious
Be playful! Be goofy!—it brings on a smile
To you and those around, for at least half a mile!"

—DIANE PIENTA

"If You Can'T See God in All, You Can'T See God at All."

— YOGI BHAJAN

Ah, those people who push our buttons. The people we judge and make wrong, certain they're on the wrong side of the political, social, vaccine debate—can we see God in them? Can we see Goddess in the angry drunk stumbling down the street cursing and smashing a bottle? Can I see God in my mother in a demented rage accusing me of stealing from her? This is God? Seems pretty demonic.

And yet. Don't we all have our dark sides? Who reading this has never done something they were deeply ashamed of afterward? You are light and God-filled regardless. We are not the worst thing we've ever done.

Our spirit, our God-force, our inner being, is always present, even though our personalities can create a cloud cover over our spirit. But what we focus on grows, and so we can grow our own light and look for it in others.

Maybe this is the ultimate gift—to interact with someone's light when their behavior is not aligned with their spirit, their God-force;

when they're really infuriating us. God knows I'm grateful for that act of grace when someone bestows it on me, when I'm granted the benefit of the doubt and forgiveness when I'm unkind or mean or just acting stupid.

Here's a cosmic twist about the quote itself. It's attributed to Yogi Bhajan. Yogi Bhajan was a spiritual teacher who brought his version of Kundalini Yoga to the United States, and was the spiritual director of Healthy Happy Holy Organization, with three hundred centers in thirty-five countries. His mission was to spread a path of elevated awareness, to contribute to a world of peace and social justice, and he impacted thousands of people. After his death, he was accused of sexual abuse by hundreds of his female followers. So now, what do you think of this quote? Do you discard it? Do you think less of this vignette, this book, because it's included here? Or can you consider that this human being violated his power, seriously hurt others, and is still capable of inspiring others to the light? Is that possible?

Marva Collins was a substitute teacher who was so successful at educating poor Black students in her challenging 1970s Chicago neighborhood that she was asked by two presidents to be a candidate for U.S. secretary of education (both of which she declined in favor of teaching students, one at a time). When a student behaved poorly, Marva's "punishment" was to have the student write all of the reasons they were too good to behave that way, from A to Z. I am admirable. I am beautiful. And so forth. If the behavior happened again, you got the same "punishment," except you couldn't use the same words. Her success rate is legendary.

What if we interacted with each other this way? When someone is unkind, can we shift from "You're an A-hole?" to "You're too beautiful to behave like this?" Can we help each other see our own goodness and act from that place? Can we remind ourselves of how beautiful we are? What if you write a list right now from A to Z of everything that's wonderful about *you*?

It sounds like that could make a magical world. Let's try.

Life Said, "I'm Going To Make You Happy, but First, I'm Going To Make You Strong."

I met Lori at the John C. Campbell Folk School one summer. The John C. Campbell Folk School is on a magical piece of land deep in the Great Smoky Mountains and offers weeklong immersions in almost every art and craft imaginable in a community life that transforms people. Really.

Lori was in the midst of a protracted, acrimonious divorce and had a six-month wait before her court date. She packed up a van, didn't tell anyone where she was going—including her grown children—drove to the Folk School, and headed straight for the blacksmithing studio.

In the hot, sooty forge all week, most nights and more than a few weekends, Lori hammered steel into gorgeous works of art. She'd done some smithing before, but nothing like this. The idea of sitting around for six months worrying and waiting for her court date made forty-plus hours a week in the forge look like a vacation. Lori's focus was on creativity and making beautiful, handmade things.

I met her about four months into her six-month escapade, and we'd laugh and talk in the dining hall. She showed us the gorgeous metal art she created, then told us about the big project she was working on—a full-suit Wonder Woman outfit meticulously hammered out of metal. Fascinated, I asked what she was going to do with it. "Wear it to court!", she said as we all burst out laughing.

Without missing a beat, Lori declared, "Life said, 'I'm going to make you happy, but first, I'm going to make you strong.'"

Lori seems to have figured out the magic formula for happiness:

1. Do something you love. Every day.
2. Use your creative gifts to make beauty.
3. Use your hands.
4. Surround yourself with like-minded community.
5. Be in community. Laugh in community.
6. Step away, literally or metaphorically, enough to get a different perspective on your worry, enough that you can even get a sense of humor going about it.

7. Do some physical work every day. Be active. Move your body, ideally in different way. Build different muscles—in your body and in your brain.

8. Chase joy. And magic. And fun.

When life inevitably deals one of her testing blows, few of us can immerse ourselves in the art studio for six months. But this refocus on creativity and beauty when the chips are down is a powerful antidote to fear and worry.

I don't know about you, but I find it hard to turn away from the problem when I'm stuck in the middle of it. My brain spins, trying to figure out ways to resolve it, as I simultaneously try not to think about it in the middle of the night. But it's darn near impossible to worry about something when you're tending a coal forge and hammering red-hot steel. Or sewing, or working with clay, or . . . What is it that you love to do with your hands?

I've experienced—and maybe you have, too—that what doesn't kill us really does make us stronger. But we make ourselves the strongest when we can turn away from the problem, if just for a smidge, and focus our energy on doing what we love.

What makes you strong?

The Power of And

Do you say "But . . ." a lot?

I didn't realize how much I said "But . . ." until I started noticing.

You know: "I'd love to find a new home in the country with beautiful land and community, *but* I'm not sure where to look", "*but* the market is insane right now", "*but* I'm afraid it might feel isolating", "*but* what if I don't love it; I don't have a ton of energy to keep moving and setting up new homes."

In other words, fear.

And is a refreshing and friendly antidote to *but*.

And is inclusive.

And is pregnant with possibilities.

And is FUN!

And gives an escape route to an uncomfortable or frightening situation.

But stops us in our tracks.

And encourages us to be curious, to explore.

But is depressive.

And is expansive.

Let's try it. I'd love to find a new home with beautiful land that I love *and* it could be really fun to just look in a bunch of different places to see what calls to me, *and* so what if the market is insane, you never know unless you look, *and* I'm good at joining groups and finding my tribe no matter where I go, *and* if I don't love it, I'll chalk it up to experience, move on, and find something else. Wow! I just excited myself.

Is there something you're considering and are stopped? What if you write out a paragraph first with your *buts* and then with your *ands*. See if you aren't just a little more enthusiastic.

I'd really like to write a book *but* what if it's a flop, *but* I don't know how.

Ok. I'd really like to write a book *and* I love to write *and* it will be fun and fulfilling to do no matter if anyone reads or likes it *and* plenty of people write books, so I can ask for help and have fun doing it.

What's the worst that could happen? You're holding the answer to that question in your hand.

189

The Drop-Dead Game

About fifteen years ago, I invented the Drop-Dead Game and invited my husband to play.

Lest you are completely appalled at how this sounds, please let me explain.

We'd been together for about eighteen years, and as is often the case with couples, our lives had become so intertwined that it was sometimes difficult to see what was my life, what was his life, and what was our life.

Trying to answer the question "What do I want?" was often clouded by wondering what my husband would like or if it would fit into our life together. He likes the ocean; I like land. He loves rich French foods and wines; I like brown rice and vegetables. We both love nature, tending land, traveling, and sharing delicious home-cooked meals with others.

I wondered, how does one approach the question "What do I want?" while navigating coupledom? I started to think about what I'd do if I were single. Which after eighteen years of being attached at the hip takes a little imagination.

I asked him one day, "What would you do if I dropped dead tomorrow?" His answer was immediate and unequivocal. "I'd sell the house and move onto a boat." Wow. Ok. Then we asked me what I would do if Dave dropped dead tomorrow. My answer came quickly, too: I'd sell this big house and find a smaller home and community closer to nature. Maybe I'd study yoga or some other modality for six months or a year.

We looked at each other in surprise. We'd both sell the house, and yet this was the first time it had even come up in conversation. We had spent twelve years in a labor of love restoring that house, and it had become a part of us like an appendage we hadn't questioned. In imagining what our lives would be like if we had total freedom, all kinds of possibilities seemed present.

So why is this often not the case when we're in a relationship? Yes, there are joint responsibilities around children and family, and many choices and compromises need to be made as a couple for the good of the whole. How, then, do we nurture our individual souls and feed our hearts at the same time?

It's so clichéd to say we all know we're going to die, but really, how many of us actually behave as though we're only here on this beautiful planet for practically a nanosecond? Do our choices really reflect that?

I'll never forget my eighty-eight-year-old father lamenting mournfully one afternoon before he died, "Where did all the years go?"

What do you long to do? What's your joy? Is there one step you can take toward this dream today?

It's Never Too Late

I saw this billboard on the side of a bus just as it pulled away. "It's Never Too Late!" the bus shouted at me in life-sized letters, seconds after I had wondered (if I'm honest, I'd say regretted) that I had left it until it was "too late" to . . . write a book, start a coaching practice, create a magical land sanctuary, and on and on. The universe plants signs for us everywhere if we look, no?

Julia Cameron of *The Artist's Way* tells how some of her students, stuck in the it's-too-late game, lament, "Do you know how old I'll be by the time I [*fill in the blank: learn to play the piano, be competent at woodworking, paint well, write a book*]?" Cheekily, Julia responds, "The same age you'll be if you don't!"

Are there projects you wished you had done? Dreams you wished you had chased? Do you tend to focus on the fact that you didn't do them and that they seem out of reach now? Do you focus on what you did or didn't do? Or do you greet the day with joy about what's possible *now*?

Polly Hill was a gardener who decided to plant an arboretum from a seed—at the age of fifty. Taking over the care of her family's farm on Martha's Vineyard, the seacoast island off the coast of Massachusetts, later in life, Polly was practical, curious, and determined. And she followed her heart's delight. Polly didn't just inspire gardeners, she encouraged anyone who wanted to change their life—*at any age*. Polly is quoted as saying, "Fifty is a great age to try something new." Polly died at the age of one hundred, but today, the Polly Hill Arboretum on the Vineyard grows strong and continues to inspire.

How often we sabotage ourselves by saying "should have, could have, would have." What if we take off those sunglasses and look through a crystal-clear lens of what might be created *now*.

In our modern world that pushes for immediate results, get-it-now and get-it-fast, radical incrementalism is a gentle antidote to the overwhelming question of how we achieve an end result or a big dream. It's the act of taking small, thoughtful steps each day, steps that lead to unimagined opportunities and unforeseen results.

I've been inspired lately by people like Polly Hill, people playing with long-haul creativity without being attached to the results. Sure there are things we'd like to achieve, but it's having fun in this now moment where the magic lies.

Chuck Blethen, a zesty, feisty, eighty-one-year-old started planting

Jewel of the Blue Ridge, his mountaintop teaching vineyard outside Marshall, North Carolina, at the age of sixty-seven, propagating and disseminating native, cold-hardy muscadine grapes to be a new economically viable replacement crop for the tobacco fields that had stretched across those mountains for centuries.

At eighty-one, Chuck says he's in it for the long haul. His curiosity and enthusiasm for life is infectious—like the pizza oven he built himself, explaining that he carried a notebook around for three years researching what worked and what didn't in pizza ovens before building his own gorgeous jewel-box of a pizza oven himself. Plus he teaches knife throwing and axe throwing, or he'll teach you about Scottish Highland steers, who I learned will die of loneliness if you just have one, since they are highly social beings. Chuck brings an energy and inspiration to life and living that's just delicious to be around. Friends, we all have this capability, no matter what our age.

When it's tempting to squash a dream by saying, "Should have done that five or ten or twenty years ago" or to fall into the trap of thinking that life's circumstances are too hard to shift now, here's something to consider: if in five or ten years you looked back at this moment, what would you want to be able to say about this time? Maybe that you jumped in with both feet and learned that the water wasn't as cold as you thought? Maybe that you had a ball?

After all, you'll be the same age whether you do it or not.

"Whatever it is that stirs your soul,
listen to that. Everything else is just noise."

—NICOLE LYONS

Nature Must Be So Disappointed If We Are Not Dazzled At Least Ten Times a Day

How often do you fall into bed thinking "Just another day" instead of "Wow! [*Fill in the blank*] was so amazing today!"?

I am looking out the big, dirty windows of my temporary, make-shift writing studio onto an overcast, cold, winter-gray, dirty urban landscape. The whole world looks like a sad, monotone, sepia painting. Ear-splitting ambulance sirens and diesel trucks rumble by the neon Domino's Pizza sign across the street as I write this, and I decide it's time to practice what I preach.

Hmmm. How am I dazzled *right now*?

Ok, I'm writing with a goose quill pen cut by hand into the most exquisite writing instrument, dipping into ink made from walnut shells, which is how our ancestors wrote for millennia, on beautiful, thick, white paper that feels silky smooth and helps the ink flow. A bird, a tree, and some nuts are all here, allowing me to write something that you are now reading. That's dazzling!

But wait. I just raised my eyes above the grime and noise to see a flock of thirty or so pigeons perched on the roof of the building across the street. They hang out for a bit, then one gives the signal, and they all fly together in the most dramatic and synchronized formation, swooping and looping round until they land once again in their hangout spot. What are they doing?! Whatever it is, they look super cool doing it. It's dazzling, really.

What's dazzling in your life right now?

The Anxiety Is The Ego Trying To Assert Itself.
The Calm, Clear, Still Lake of Light
Is Who You Really Are. Be That.

I used to read words like these above and initially feel very calm and lovely. I'd usually read them after an expansive morning meditation, mentally floating, feet-up in that calm, clear, still lake. Ahhh. Yes, I *am* that calm, clear, still lake of light. Yes indeed, I am.

Then I'd go into the kitchen, and my husband would have the radio blaring, and the phone would start ringing super early with clients, and we'd be out of oatmeal, and I'd realize that I didn't have any clean underwear, and then I assure you, I was certainly not that calm, clear, still lake of light any longer. I was a tsunami. And I would think, "Where did those words ever come from?"

Life. Maybe some of you have been practicing being that calm, clear, still lake for a while now, and maybe you're pretty good at it. Maybe you're new at this and you're saying, "If I could be that calm, clear, still lake of light, don't you think I'd just be that whenever I wanted?!"

Don't you wish there were a button you could push when you're in the tsunami? A secret formula? Lots of books and teachers say they have the formula for Success! Happiness! Abundance! The Best Life You Can Imagine! Don't get me wrong. I secretly love these books. And I suppose maybe there is a secret formula. Maybe the secret formula is practice. And remembering.

Viktor Frankl said, "Between stimulus and response there is a space. In that space is our power to choose our response. In our response lies our growth and our freedom." It's not always a big space, but I've experienced that as we practice, we can start to play with the length of that space. And the more often we choose the calm, clear, still lake of light—which *is* who we really are—the more we are that, the more our reactions and words and inner peace reflect that calm lake of light.

But, ah. Remembering. Remembering all these practices is a whole other animal.

Remembering to take that pause between the stimulus and the response. Well, there's the magic.

I asked my chiropractor yesterday why one tiny area in my back keeps going out. "What's the root cause of that?" I wondered. She gave me a general explanation—we're rounded over our phones and computers so much of the time and our shoulders aren't well aligned. It creates poor posture and strain, especially in our middle back. "You just have to remember to keep your shoulders back," she said. Of course! So much to remember in this life!

The quote about being the lake of light came to me during a dark period. A period when I wasn't the calm, clear, still lake of light. I won't bore you with the details. But at one point, something happened—a stimulus—and I was overcome with grief and despair. Somehow, through the tears, I had the wherewithal to raise my eyes to I-don't-know-who and demand, "I need divine intervention NOW into this situation." The crying stopped immediately, and these words flooded my consciousness, "the anxiety is the ego trying to assert itself; the calm, clear, still lake of light is who you really are—be that."

Suddenly, I just knew that I was the calm, clear, still lake. And that it was up to me to be that. Whatever it took.

In that space, and in choosing a new response, I took my attention off myself, invited our friends over for dinner, and had fun playing hide-and-seek with their kids in our new apartment. I knew that laughing would break the static. I knew that who I am in the world is someone who creates fun community gatherings, someone who loves to cook delicious food and share it with others. The situation hadn't changed, I just needed to change and be who I really am in this world.

When you are that calm, clear, still lake of light, who are you?

Don't Live like Nobody's Watching. Live like Your Ancestors Are Watching!

Who are your ancestors? What are your family stories? Are they written down or told over a holiday dinner table? Are they lost?

My great-grandmother came to the United States from Lithuania around 1900. She had very little money, no English, a set of infant twins (one of whom died and had to be thrown overboard on the steerage journey over the Atlantic), a husband who worked and got sick in the coal mines and then had three more children. One daughter died at nineteen; the other twin died in a tragic car accident before he was fifty. And yet in the midst of the Depression, she and her husband managed to buy a farm and proceeded to create a good, simple life. The few pictures we have, show her looking serene on her land as she lived into her nineties. My Goddess, this woman is resilient!

There's a lot of talk these days about clearing out old ancestral patterns we've inherited that no longer serve us or that actually keep us from thriving, and God knows, I'm all in favor of that. And, I'm interested in honoring the extraordinary qualities our ancestors exhibited, knowing that those qualities, too, are imbedded in us to use, like superpowers, when we need them.

When I'm boo-hooing about some of the challenges I'm facing, I think about what my great-grandmother would have done to assuage her broken heart or loneliness or grief.

She would have done what women have done for millennia after war or in desperate situations. She would have gotten up and fed the animals and baked the bread. She would have sewed the clothes, collected the eggs, and dug the potatoes. She would have collected scraps for the quilt, tended her bees, and saved her seeds for next year's food. She may have had to haul her grief-stricken self from bed in the morning, but she got up and made new life in the new day. She died before I was born, so how do I know this? Because I'm here now to tell the story.

I hope she's watching over me with her strong resilient strength and that she's proud of how I'm behaving in the world. I know she's rooting for me when I pick myself up and reach for the light, when I make beauty out of darkness.

If I sense that she (and the other ancestors) are watching, I'm a lot more careful to be my best self, in the words of positive psychology. I wonder what she'd think about positive psychology.

How about you? Who are your ancestors? What are their stories? I bet they were resilient. How do I know this? Because you are here, now, reading this.

Won't it be fun to watch our descendants—either our children or our creative projects—two hundred years from now and see how our lives continue to live through them? Won't it be fun to root for them?

What are all the extraordinary qualities your ancestors possessed? Do you know in your bones that you too possess these qualities?

What would you do if you knew your ancestors were watching?

Make a delicious bone broth from your ancestors' stories. Let this nourish you, your descendants, and your creations.

Everything in My Life Is a Gift— Everything and Everyone, No Exceptions

Not long ago, I broke my ankle. Gift? Really?

I live in a third floor walkup. My husband was out of the country. We were new in the neighborhood, and I didn't know my neighbors. It was winter, and the sidewalks were icy.

But here's the weird thing. Less than ten minutes before the break, I was talking to a friend about how I was having trouble beginning to write this book. I said, "I've been going in so many different directions this year, maybe I just need to have my plane grounded so I can root-in and write."

Pow! Universe delivered that one immediately. Careful what you wish for and all that. And it was the best gift. I slowed down to a near standstill, canceling all my activities and travel, which created perfect time, space, and structure to . . . write.

I had also just asked the universe the week before to open my heart wide to experience big love, connection, and true friendship after a year of heartbreak. Hours after the accident, I had a tsunami of love and friendship as my community rallied 'round and brought food, crutches, prescriptions, rides, visits, and big love. I felt so cared for, loved, appreciated, and connected. It was such a gift.

In *Transform Your Life through Your Handwriting*, Dr. Vimala Rodgers, whose words open this chapter, explains how writing our letters in an empowering way can help rewire our brains to cultivate the spiritual qualities we want to develop. By choosing a letter and writing it along with its soul quality, mindfully, for forty days (the approximate time it takes to establish a habit), we can bring the essence of that quality into our lives. By the way, the soul quality of the first letter of your name gives you insight into both your greatest gift and your greatest challenge.

Do you ever look back at a particularly difficult period and notice that there's a gift or a teaching in it? A silver lining? Maybe it made you stronger, or pushed you to pursue your passion, or helped you to get clear on your boundaries. Writing Gg and its soul quality (*Everything in My Life Is a Gift—Everything and Everyone, No Exceptions*) for months now has me so curious about anything and everything that would have been frustrating or super upsetting before. In almost any difficult situation, my response is to now ask, pretty quickly, "Hmm, what's the gift in this?" I tell you, it makes life kind of fascinating.

As Vimala would say, don't believe me, try it for yourself! Vimala walks her own talk. Living through some extremely painful life experiences, she maintains her teaching that "everything is a gift, no exceptions."

And as Ellen Tadd often taught, "Life viewed from a human perspective can sometimes seem tragic, but viewed from a spiritual perspective suddenly gets very interesting."

Who and what are the gifts in your life today?

"Let Us Give Thanks for Unknown Blessings Already on The Way."

—QUAKER MEALTIME BLESSING

Not long ago, I found myself without a home. It's true, I thought it would be fun to sell our house without another to "see what would happen," Goddess bless my husband. Without a stable home base and no clear direction of where to move to, no clear purposeful work direction, the recent death of my mother, a renewed diagnosis of cancer for my husband, a pandemic going on (oh, for heaven's sake), and some long-term friendships reaching their end, it felt incredibly empty.

Have you been there?

Despite all of my previous declarations that I loved making friends with the unknown, this was the real deal. The universe had called my bluff. Every day, I asked Spirit, "Where would you have me go? What's mine to do today?" Sometimes the answers were clear as bell. Often there seemed to be silence.

It was a time of groping my way in the dark, practicing everything I'm preaching to see magic and beauty everywhere, even as I wondered what I was doing on this earth. But friends, it was often hard.

This quote reached me just in time, a reminder that blessings are constantly, every second, zooming toward us, intent on delighting us if we can just get out of the way and open our eyes.

Have you ever looked back on a difficult (or any) period, three or four or ten years later and marveled, "I could never have planned this working out so perfectly"? I imagined myself, five years from now, looking back, laughing and saying, "*What* was I so worried about?"

To turn this equation on its head, to anticipate with delight the gifts and blessings streaking their way to us like the light that left a star years ago and is making its' way to us so we see the magic of its light many years later, well, that's some kind of powerful.

What kinds of unknown blessings might be on their way to you right now?

Who Inspires You?

As I sit down to write this, I learn that Paul Farmer, the extraordinary Harvard doctor and humanitarian who devoted his life to tirelessly delivering health care to the world's poorest people, died yesterday. Reading just a few lines of his obituary, I'm overcome by the astonishing impact he's had on the world and on the lives of millions, and it's enough for all of my petty concerns to immediately drop away as I'm impelled to find more ways to be of service. Now.

Sometimes we think if we don't have the right degree or are not connected in the right places, we can't make an impact in this world.

Consider Nannette Canniff. Back in the 1980s, Nannette was a working class mother of ten, married to her high school sweetheart, attending church in one of the poorest neighborhoods in Quincy, Massachusetts, when the church decided to do a walk for hunger. It was a simple walk, and they raised some funds. They decided to donate half the funds to the Home for Children in Haiti but were told that they had to hand deliver the funds. So off to Haiti they went, led by Nannette and the parish priest.

When they arrived, they were sent to a small village in the remote mountains. Nannette describes being stunned by the poverty, by people living in huts, not houses, and said, "We need to help these people." Asking the community what they'd do to improve their lives, the community said they'd build and staff a health clinic to help the sick. And so Nannette quickly organized ways to raise the money for it, then worked alongside the people in Haiti to build and staff it. Six years later, she and her group incorporated as a charity, and for the first twenty-four years, they operated it out of her home.

Thirty years later, and this one-room health clinic is now the largest care center in southern Haiti, treating more than 130,000 patients each year and employing five hundred employees, ninety-eight-percent of whom are Haitian. All this from an open heart and an initial desire to make a contribution to others, no matter how small.

How easy it might have been to go back to raising ten children, with all the details and busyness that goes along with that. How easy to say the problem was just too big to make a difference. How easy to say that we personally don't have the resources to make a difference.

How awe-inspiring to know of people who live their lives in service to something grander than themselves. I tell you, just reading and writing about these extraordinary people opens my heart wide, enabling me to see how I can be more of service. Being in the presence, even just by reading, of extraordinary people can touch that part of us that is equally extraordinary and is maybe eager to step into some new roles in this world of ours.

Who are you inspired by? What about them inspires you? What if you took a moment to write a few lines about the inspiration they evoke? Or to read something about their life that reminds you of your own gifts of greatness?

The world needs our gifts—*now*. You have everything you need right now to make a difference and serve what you came here to serve.

What if we all tapped into our own gifts and offered them to the world with open hearts?

What a world that would be.

What's your gift that the world needs now?

You Are The One
Who Calls in Happiness and Joy

Wake up, My Child, come out to play
Time to stop hiding and trying to pray
To understand Life's will for you
To understand what you're "supposed" to do
Bloom where you're planted
Blossom and grow
That's all you really need to know
Take root where you are, on this beautiful earth
Release now your fears, compost them all into dirt

Dust off your wings, polish your shoes
Sharpen your pencil, broaden your views.
Dip in your paintbrush, can your tomatoes
Cook up some soup, play with mixing life's flavors.

Be the Magic

Walk the dog, play the guitar
Do some yoga, plan trips all afar
Sit down at the piano, learn how to sew
Oh wait 'til you see, just how far you will go.

To tennis, to pottery, to woodworking delights
Enjoy howling at the moon on those shimmering,
glimmering, clear full-moon nights
Play with your friends, play with your art,
But whatever you do, you must follow your heart

Awaken Dear Child, our artist within,
And bloom where you're planted…

Come, let us begin.

—DIANE PIENTA

Sit Under The Heat Lamp of Clarity

How is it for you when you're confused?

Confused is different from "not knowing". "Not knowing" has a potentially curious quality to it; there's some excitement in the unknown, even if it might generate some fear. "Not knowing" offers the possibility of learning something new, of expansion. "I don't know" is a powerfully honest statement and can grant us the inspiration to discover and explore. "I don't know" can lead to "Let's find out!" It can be a powerful place to be.

Confusion, on the other hand, can be a dark, swirling energy that leaves us disoriented. It has us doubting ourselves and others, second-guessing our choices, and spiraling us into rumination and fear.

A few years ago I decided to make friends with the unknown. It took a little cultivating to be comfortable in each other's presence, and like any relationship, we had our ups and downs. Our brains don't like change, and the degree of the unknown and how out of our comfort zone we are can determine our level of excitement or fear. But when I can just sit comfortably with "I don't know," curiosity starts knocking, and the fear subsides.

We're taught in this modern culture of ours to know, or at least to sound and look like we have, the answers. "I don't know" can be seen as weak, when in fact, it generates trust and is the cornerstone of art, creativity, and invention.

But confusion. Confusion has me going left then right, up then down, turning three ways at once, compounding the problem. Confusion is like a restless sea, a dangerous place to navigate.

Decisions made from a place of confusion are rarely wise and often lead to even more confusion and second-guessing, keeping the cycle going. Confusion sucks energy. Clarity energizes.

A soothing antidote to confusion is to sit under the heat lamp of clarity. Confusion has a swirling, fluid, liquid quality about it. She's murky, foggy, muddy. Clarity has a drier quality to it. Like a crystal-clear day, one of those bright days when the humidity is low, the air is dry, and we can see for miles. That's the quality of mind I'm after.

So how to access it? When my head is swirling and it's not clear which way is up, I imagine a giant, golden heat lamp above my head, radiating a golden beam of clarity into every atom and cell of my body, every inch, soaking up that moisture of confusion. You can think of it like one of those big hairdryers in the salon that comes down over your head, radiating clarity into your brain and enveloping your whole being in a warm, clear, powerful transmission of lucidity.

Clarity doesn't mean we suddenly have the answers, but it does give us a settled and expanded sense of being from which we can become more comfortable with "I don't know." And from a comfortable place of "I don't know," we're often led to a brilliant solution.

There are lots of ways to access clarity. Some people do it with prayer or meditation or a walk in the woods. Sometimes I walk around all day in this light beam of clarity while breathing very deeply into my belly and keeping my eyes still. It follows me around like a spotlight, encasing my body in a golden funnel of clarity. Maybe it's a play on the Charlie Brown character Pig Pen, who walks around in his personal dust cloud that he calls the "dust of ancient civilizations," while his mind and conscience are clear.

Of course, you can sit under the heat lamp of clarity anytime, not only in confusion. Regular treatments can help confusion from settling in in the first place.

What if you take just five minutes before you turn the page and see what it's like for you under this heat lamp of clarity?

"One Positive Thought Creates Millions of Positive Vibrations."

—JOHN COLTRANE

Who do you like to be around? People with mostly positive thoughts or people with mostly negative thoughts?

What would others say about you—that you're a person with mostly positive thoughts or mostly negative thoughts?

Some studies suggest that we think approximately seventy thousand thoughts a day. Holy cow. Despite what we might hope, even for those of us who see ourselves as cheerful, upbeat beings, a large percentage of our thoughts are negative; some say eighty-percent of our thoughts tend to the negative bias. I tracked my thoughts for a week. As a self-proclaimed harbinger of positivity, I was horrified to see my results.

I watched as, unconsciously, many of my thoughts ran toward the negative. From beating myself up for not doing as good a job as I wanted, to assuming the worst of someone, to ruminating over an old conversation.

You can try this yourself right now if you want. What if you put this book down, sit quietly for ten minutes, and watch what comes in. Don't try to think any specific thoughts; just see what comes in.

Did you do it?

What happened?

How do you feel?

Ok. What if you take another five minutes and think of someone or something in your life. Actively think of all the things you absolutely love and appreciate about this person or this thing. Really shower them with glowing, positive thoughts. Feel the emotions and appreciation, as though you were head-over-heels in love.

Did you do it?

What happened?

How do you feel?

Now how about this: how about thinking of someone who annoys you a little. I don't mean someone who is totally pushing your buttons, just someone who is, you know, annoying. What if you actively think of all the things you like about them, all the good parts of this person you usually overlook as you think, "So. Annoying." Just five minutes! You can do it! Again, really feel the emotion and appreciation for this person.

Did you do it?

What happened?

How do you feel?

Friends, this joyful, glowing, uplifted feeling is accessible whenever you choose it. I know, when we're in the thick of the darkness, this often doesn't seem possible. We can feel like we're being hijacked into fear or negativity. Positive emotions have a calming effect on our nervous system; so not only does it feel better to focus on the positive, it makes us healthier.

You may be saying, "Well of course, Diane. I know this. But how do I stop the negative thoughts?" One thought at a time. Practice! You'll get good at it.

The games and practices in this little book are all about shifting into a positive mindset. The next time you find yourself going down the rabbit hole, put some music on and get into a different groove. Dance around; where the body goes, the mind will follow. Call a friend (one who's also committed to upgrading their conversation!), and do something you absolutely love. Say "STOP!" You'll figure out what's best for you.

Just one thought at a time. Not all at once. Be easy on yourself! But that one thought you shift—it *will* make a difference.

What if you wrote a list now of all the delicious ways you want to feel?

Sing Your Words!

Do you sing?

Do you ever notice that it's hard to be dark while singing at the same time? Try it sometime. When you're feeling down, what happens if you sing one of your favorite songs for just five minutes? Not just listening but singing along.

Singing stimulates our vagus nerve, which as the longest nerve in the body connects our brains to various organs. In fact, *vagus* means "wandering" in Latin, as this nerve travels all over the body influencing our fight-or-flight response, breathing, digestive function, and heart rate. By stimulating the vagus nerve, you send a message to your body that it's time to relax and de-stress, relieving anxiety and calming your brain. Singing is one of the easiest ways to stimulate this nerve by sending musical vibrations through us. Who couldn't use more good vibrations these days?

Once upon a time, my husband and I would sing our words to each other. "Pass the butter" could be sung in an operatic style. "What should we have for dinner?" might be queried in a twangy country melody. "Who's walking the dog?" might be delivered with my Polish-princess accented tune. We weren't singers. We were newlyweds, we were goofy, and it was just fun. Little did we know that we were stimulating our vagus nerves, so it wasn't only the honeymoon period that was feeling good. We were calming our brains and nervous systems at the same time.

Never was the power of music and singing more apparent than in my mother's assisted living home. Located in a small town in Pennsylvania with a large Polish population, her home brought in live music once a week. On her first day, the featured gig was Stanky and the Coal Miners. We all filed into the performance space as the hard-core dementia residents were wheeled to the front row in their wheelchairs. These were the people who were no longer speaking, feeding themselves, or engaging. Their heads hung, their eyes seemed lifeless. For many of them, Polish was their first language.

My heart was sad as I watched them come in, and I wondered if the music would bring any pleasure. I needn't have worried, because as soon as Stanky cranked up an old-fashioned polka sung in Polish, every single one of them had their feet tapping in perfect rhythm while their lips mouthed the words in sync with Stanky and the band. Somehow, the music bypassed the no-longer-cognitive portions of their brains and activated something much deeper and primal in them.

When my own mother slipped into advanced Alzheimer's and she was no longer able to speak, feed herself, or recognize us, she would hum, nearly nonstop, as do many dementia patients. She didn't hum or sing pre-dementia, but some primal part of her knew this would calm her system.

A wise woman once offered me this advice: "The quickest way we lose our power is when we stop singing and dancing. The quickest way to get our power back is to start singing and dancing."

I've been humming the whole time I'm writing this. Yes, the situation in the world seems dire, another friend just tested positive for Covid, our living situation is still uncertain, but the last hour of humming has me feeling a little more peaceful in the world. And if I can be more peaceful, I can radiate that out in this world of ours. And maybe this will create a little more peace in the world. Will you join me?

"The only thing better than singing is more singing." —ELLA FITZGERALD

What's Your Story?

If you just met someone and they asked, "So, what's your story?" what would you tell them? What would you focus on?

Would you focus on facts—"My name is Diane, married, lived in Boston for thirty years, worked in business for two decades, now writing and starting a new career"?

Would you focus on others in your life—"I have five nieces and nephews who are super fun, ranging from seven years old to twenty-seven"?

Would you focus on what's wrong—"I really don't like the noise and the traffic where I live, but I haven't found anywhere else that feels good to move to, so I'm still in Boston"?

Would you focus on what brings you joy—"I love my community of friends and my yoga community. I love the vibrancy of the city combined with the amazing green spaces in this town. I love to gather people together with delicious food in beautiful places in nature. I love writing, playing my fiddle, felting, and climbing trees"?

Stories are the way we comprehend the world and our place in it. We're storytelling beings, after all. When the stories we tell about our lives are comprehensible, manageable, and meaningful, we have a greater tendency toward happiness, health, and resiliency. When our life stories fixate on what's wrong, we're more susceptible to the depression/anxiety end of the scale. Our stories really are self-fulfilling prophecies.

Positive psychology has a method called "re-storying"—taking an old disempowering story we've been telling about ourselves and rewriting it in a way that gives us back our power. It's not whitewashing the truth; it's simply shifting our focus from what stinks to what was positive about this experience. For me, it was shifting from "I haven't had meaningful work in five years" to " I've had the incredible opportunity to explore art, music, mysticism, spirituality, alternative healing modalities, positive psychology, and the world, and now I get to share this with others."

Recently, I was asked to answer this question: "Looking forward twenty years, I am attending a function where someone is giving a speech about me. What do I want them to say?"

I want them to say that I'm kind and that my love for this incredibly beautiful world we live in is infectious. I want them to say that I'm someone who finds magic and beauty everywhere and that my curiosity is insatiable. I want them to say that their lives are better because of my presence in it. I want them to say that I create beauty and have a peaceful heart that's easy to be around. I want them to say that I take the time to be with people, that I acknowledge others' light and gifts and help others find peace, purpose, and fun in their lives.

I want them to say that I'm a thankful person who follows and lives my joy—every day. That I find delight in the smallest things. That I love to laugh and be playful and am deeply spiritual at the same time. That I love to make music and dance with others, love juicy, deep conversations, am a good friend to others. That I love to make things with my hands, love to learn, and love to share what I've learned.

I want them to say that I help others align with their highest selves, that I inspire them to take risks and break old patterns and that I do this myself. I want them to say that my books positively changed lives. I want them to say that I'm a gatherer of people, that I cocreate enchanting spaces on the land for people to soak in nature's beauty and play together in magical ways to feel whole and content. That I'm brave and inspire others to take risks to follow their dreams. And that I'm both a generous and grateful soul. I want them to say that I'm a masterful fiber artist who creates beautiful works of art and clothing from felt and wool and deerskin. I want them to say that I welcome everyone into my clan. I want them to say that I'm a little goofy and follow my unconventional dreams. I want them to say that I help open hearts to the healing power of nature in deep, powerful, and fun ways and that I cook lots of delicious food and invite everyone to my table.

Phew. I better get busy! Well, that's a lot more fun than my story earlier this morning in which someone might have said, "She was dark and doubtful about her ability to manifest her creativity in the world."

Which of these stories energizes you? Which deflates you like a sad balloon?

There are so many people today teaching us to visualize the future we want to see, to hold this vision in our heart and to really feel it. There's so much power in not only visualizing but writing your future into existence, giving us the power to make it so. We're creating it either way, with a story that either excites us or contracts us.

What story do you want to be told about you in twenty years? What if you start writing a few sentences now?

*"It's like everyone tells a story about themselves
inside their own head. Always. All the time. That story
makes you what you are. We build ourselves out of that story."*

——PATRICK ROTHFUSS

"There is no greater agony than bearing an untold story inside you."

——MAYA ANGELOU

There's Power in Completion

How are you at completing things?

There's power in completing projects or tasks. There's that great positive emotion we can experience when we accomplish even something small. We can actually get an endorphin rush, or an enormous sense of pride when we achieve something challenging. Our unfinished projects, on

231

the other hand, can dangle over our heads like little swords. Completing a project gives us energy. Incomplete projects can drain our energy as they sit blinking at us across the room, waiting for us to do something about them.

As a rehabilitated perfectionist über-Virgo recovering from the disease to please, my tendency toward organization and completion can be a bit ferocious—as long as it's for others or a group. Assign me a group project with a deadline, and I'm your girl.

So why has this same devotion to completion been missing in the creative projects I'd like to share with the world?

Take for instance this book you're now reading. For the past week, more than three-quarters of the way through, I'm about to ditch the whole thing. I'm nearly at the end of the writing, and my creative juices seem to have dried up. Done. Gone. More alarming was that my initial delight and excitement in writing was gone. Finit. Kaput.

The insidious voices inside my head wouldn't stop. "No one's going to want to read this anyway." "Who do you think you're kidding? You really don't have anything worthwhile to say." And the big one: "You're not going to finish this one, either."

Ack! Time to get to the bottom of this. I've had a few big creative ideas that I began with great encouragement and feedback from others, only to have them sitting unfinished on my shelf ten years later. What's up with this?

Fortunately, legendary shame researcher Brené Brown came to the rescue. Or maybe unfortunately. Who the heck wants to talk about shame? Her book *Daring Greatly* fell into my lap just a week prior, reminding me how much courage it takes to be vulnerable, to open our hearts to the risk of rejection, failure, and humiliation. And yet to live what Brené calls a "wholehearted life" requires that we do just this while also developing "shame resiliency." I'll leave it up to Brené to illuminate all the powerful ways we can do this, as she does so compellingly yet humorously in her book.

For the record, I'm not someone who particularly likes to go around talking about shame. It seems, well, shameful, cringe-worthy. But as

Brené points out, every single person who isn't a sociopath experiences shame. And shame thrives in silence.

So I asked for some divine guidance: "What the heck does shame have to do with my completing this book?" Immediately, a college memory flooded in. I remembered being chosen as a teaching assistant for a very popular class. I had never taught before, had no training, and was taking the class myself. I was told that I'd be teaching a group of my peers the material for three out of four weeks, at which point the rock-star motivational-speaker professor would fly in and mesmerize the crowd on week four. We'd do this throughout the semester.

For my first group lesson, I was super nervous, but I thought I'd prepared more than adequately...until twelve minutes into the hour-long class, when I ran out of material. I fumbled and tried to wing it, which just made things worse. All humor and perspective left me as I panicked.

One of the guys in my class (who I later learned had been turned down for the TA position) started heckling me in front of everyone. "How did you get to be a TA for this class?" he demanded. "You're obviously not remotely qualified to be up there." You could have cut the tension with a knife as the other students watched this interaction. Wince-worthy.

It was worse than the dream where you're at school and realize you're naked. At least you wake up from that. I was at school, and I *was* naked. As he stormed out of the room and some of his posse followed, the humiliation was beyond painful.

For the next session, I prepared like a madwoman, but the tone had been set. This guy took me on, interrogating every word that came out of my mouth, continuing to belligerently ask in front of the class how I'd been chosen for the position. I sure wish I'd known about meditation and inner power back then or had the courage to ask for help. But I didn't. I was ashamed to admit that I was bombing.

Ahh. So is this why I pull back when I get close to stepping into a powerful teaching role or close to putting my creative gifts out in the world, risking vulnerability, exposure, and rejection? The internalized voice of that A-hole guy is still running the show. Until now.

I want to live, as Brené Brown calls it, wholeheartedly. Do you?

I want to be courageous about putting myself and my art out in the world, whether or not anyone likes it or even if it gets heckled. Do you?

Do you have incomplete projects insidiously asking for your attention? Maybe you want to create something and keep putting it off; maybe there's a dream you want to pursue but tell yourself you're not ready, or maybe you just want to clean up the basement. If you have no incomplete projects, you are blessed beyond words, and I am in awe of you. And if you're human, there's probably something that begs or whispers for your attention.

What keeps you from completing? What if this week you completed just one thing that's incomplete?

"Gotta Love Being in This World, Gotta Love The Mystery." —BUSC

I was hanging out with my magical, tuned-in friend Jim Busconi the other day. I had been thinking about how I love being in the calm, blissed-out state that happens when I'm deep in meditation and was thinking about people who spend years in caves meditating. "I love being in the spirit world," I said. "I can spend a lot of time there, you know?"

Busc is very tapped into spirit, and I figured he'd agree with me.

His response was wise. "Super D, you got to love being in *this* world, girl. You gotta love the world we're in now. You gotta love the mystery and the craziness and insanity and the questions, and all of it." Right on, Busc.

So I started looking at all the things that make me love being in this world. I love people. I love writing. I love painting and color. I love creating gardens and homes that I love to share with others. I love traveling to see new places. I love to share what I've learned. I love dancing and cooking delicious food for friends. I love helping others love being in this world. I love nature so much. I love synchronicity. And magic.

What do you love?

When we do what we love, we love being in this world, and surely, that's what we're here for. Not to suffer and prove we're right but to be in love with this world and to lend a helping hand to others who might be having a hard time doing that.

Maybe, this is the access to peace.

What do you love most about being in this world? What if you wrote down three things you love most, right now?

"Take Some Time from The Pursuit of Happiness Just To Be Happy." —MARTÍN PRECHTEL

What if your job today was just to be happy? Not fake-it, slap a smiley face on it happy but fall in bed at the end of day with pure joy and contentment happy?

What thoughts would you think? What would you do? Who would you hang with? What would you eat? Where would you go?

The other day I was feeling overwhelmed and even a little stressed by the amount of daily practices I do to stay grounded and peaceful and, well, happy. And no, the complete irony of this is not lost on me. Ok, twenty minutes for meditation, and will that give me enough time to get a healthy dose of outdoor time before morning yoga starts? But wait! I haven't done my three pages of morning journaling. Aaaghhh! Ridiculous.

Sometimes we're so focused on fixing what we think is wrong with ourselves, on managing our stress or anxiety, that we actually forget to stop and ask ourselves what is wonderful about this very moment.

What can we be delighted by, or interested in, or curious about, or excited about right now? Is there some action we can take that would be so much fun? Or peaceful? What could you think right now to generate happy?

This pursuit of happiness, of daily practices, of reading books (like this one!), or of striving to meet goals we think will make us happy can turn into a full-time seeking.

I find that saying thank you is one of the easiest routes into a happy mindset. I say thank you to my car for driving me around, thank you for my bright, sunny, makeshift writing studio, thank you for my computer that has become practically an appendage and is my connection to the world. What could you thank?

Dr. Sue Morter made the lovely observation that the universe is constantly showering us with gifts, but we're often too clouded in negativity to see them. Who do we like to give presents to? The person who is truly delighted and thanks us profusely or the person who doesn't even acknowledge our gift? Me, I love when I'm thanked with abundance; I can't wait to find another gift to give. Apparently, the universe does, too, because I swear, more beautiful gifts, synchronicities, and delights show up when I'm focused on saying thanks, as though the world were saying, "You thought that was great? Check *this* out!" And maybe this exchange and reciprocity with the world is our access to being happy while making the universe happy, too. You know, a little Happiness Mutual Exchange program.

Seems to me that most if not all of us would like to live each day with a little more inner peace, contentment . . . happiness.

So what if you made a list right now of the times you remember laughing so hard you nearly wet your pants or of times when you've had that delicious easy feeling of flow. Of a time you were just overwhelmed with beauty or had a deep, profound sense of satisfaction. What if you just soaked that in for a little while? Kept feeding your brain those luscious thoughts? And then thanked whatever you could find to thank.

What if you just decided to be really happy today?

"You can't find happiness, you just have to be happy without it."

—MARTÍN PRECHTEL

If I Were Here as an Enlightened Being, I Would...

- Pour love on situations that upset me.
- Laugh like crazy every day and find other people who love laughing too.
- Be so curious about everything. About all kinds of people and their stories, about how everything works—the history of everything and the whys of everything. But maybe if I was an enlightened being I would know all that already!
- Do almost everything slower.
- Be confident and excited to step into unknown roles and territory.
- Just know that everything is working out great, no matter how things looked.
- Sure as heck stop worrying.
- Play a lot more.
- Oh, and I wouldn't hold grudges.
- Do what I loved first instead of hoping there would be time and energy at the end of the day.

- Talk to more strangers.
- Know each moment, deep in my bones, that we're here so temporarily and not waste a minute being less than joyful and in awe.
- Be thrilled to be a beginner and to not know.
- Look at each moment as though I could be gone at any second.
- Be kind to people who are unkind.
- Have so much fun knowing I was capable of absolutely anything I wanted to do.

How about you? If you were here as an enlightened being, how would you be?

Do you know what? You are that.

It's Time To Be Bold

"The time is now to be bold and use your full expression—that which you know to be true. To BE your contribution. It is not to convince or to dominate but to be a flower or a tree that is opening—to be your nature. Be bold to encourage the boldness of others. There is no need to agree or have consensus. When expression is repressed, evolution is repressed."

—DIANE PIENTA

What is your bold expression?

If you're reading this, maybe you've heard this asked dozens of time before. And yet—are you fully expressing your power, creativity, and joy—that which you know to be true?

Don't wait. It won't get easier.

The world is waiting for you with open arms.

"Most of us have two lives. The life we live, and the unlived life within us."

—STEVEN PRESSFIELD

A Final Musing

"Overall, I think the main thing a musician would like to do
is give a picture to the listener of the many wonderful things that
he knows of and senses in the universe.... That's what I would like to do.
I think that's one of the greatest things you can do in life
and we all try to do it in some way. The musician's is through his music."

—JOHN COLTRANE

How do you give a picture of the many wonderful things you know of and that you sense in the universe? How do you share your incredibly magnificent gifts with the world?

Be The Magic is one way to share some of the magic I've gleaned in my short stint in this miraculous world. It's a way of painting the picture of what I sense in life. My hope is that the practices here can help you more fully access the peace, love, joy, and delight that are already in your beautiful heart. Maybe it can spark a new joyful creation in you that you'll share with us. Maybe you'll start to keep your own journal of uplifting quotes. Maybe it can help you step into new ways of thinking, new ways of being—new consciousness.

Some people seem to unabashedly and effortlessly live their gifts fully and share them with the world. Others of us fight the demons in our heads that tell us we're not ready, not good enough, or not clear enough.

Coltrane seems to have nailed it when he said, "One of the greatest things you can do in life . . . is to give a picture of the many wonderful things that [s]he knows." In other words, sharing our one-of-a-kind gifts with others.

Seems to me, tapping into our deliciously unique way of seeing the world and creatively sharing that with others is the reason we've come to this planet. It's time to strip away the old ways of thinking, the old patterns that keep us from fully expressing ourselves, our creativity, and joy in the world. Each one of us has been given a distinctive, unique gift, just like our fingerprints. Not leaving an imprint of our thumb on this world for the short time we're here seems stingy and akin to rejecting the gift itself.

A year ago, I spoke with magic-maker Rebecca Singer, who encouraged me to write this book. I explained that I'd been traveling the world, studying a bunch of different healing modalities, spirituality, art, and creativity for a few years. I felt incredibly lucky to be able to do this and a little uneasy—sheepish even—that I had this good fortune when so many others in the world were struggling. I didn't share much of what I was up to, out of this uncomfortable feeling that I should have been working instead of playing. I stayed small and off the radar. Rebecca exclaimed, "Your life is extraordinary! The only thing that should make you uncomfortable is that you're not sharing it with others!"

I submit that your life is extraordinary too. Your unique gifts are extraordinary. Your contribution is extraordinary.

Is there something that keeps you from playing full out, from being ok with making mistakes, from moving past your vulnerability and being the full contribution you came here to be? Is there something that keeps you from living your unique joy and creativity today, not waiting for tomorrow?

Is there something that keeps you from being peaceful, grateful, loving, or forgiving?

I invite you to try some of the practices in this book. Have fun playing with them. Play is the highest form of learning, after all. If nothing resonates, don't give up. Find something else that can help you shift your thinking to powerful possibility.

Doing this can be an access to peace, the kind of peace in our hearts that allows us to fall into bed at the end of the day saying, "Jeepers, that was a great day," and it's this kind of peace that ripples out into our families, our communities, and our world.

We are capable of so much more than we think.

May you always remember what a magnificent being you are and that we get to be on this grand planet for just a blink of an eye.

May you have all the encouragement you need to live fully and courageously from your heart.

And may you joyfully shine your own star so brilliantly for your time here.

With belief in your magic,
Diane

Acknowledgments

Wow! My book is complete and I can't believe what a joyful and humbling ride it's been…and, how it couldn't have happened without the help and support of my beyond—generous, supportive and creative village. A million thanks and so many blessings to you all.

First is the most deeply heartfelt gratitude to the land in the Fenway neighborhood of Boston where I live—to the Muddy River and all of her trees and birds, to the Sun who rose and set over her elegant curves and to all the beings of the land who whispered encouragement and showed me the magic again and again. I couldn't have written this book without you.

A deep acknowledgment and debt of gratitude, too, to the countless teachers and healers who generously shared their wisdom, their hearts and their love with me over the years. I am so grateful to you and the teachers who came before you.

And sometimes, we meet the most extraordinary teachers and healers, fellow-beings who have a magical ability to bridge our spirits with our human-ness. They arrive with pitchers of the coolest, most delicious water when we didn't even know we were parched. They are wise souls who transform our minds and unlock our hearts.

Two such souls—Martín Prechtel and Ellen Tadd—have been especially important to me and continue to guide my life. You are light-bringers and I am lucky beyond lucky to be your student.

To Martín Prechtel goes deeply heartfelt thanks for your beyond-generous, deliciously eloquent, love-filled school. Your teachings bend my brain, open my heart and delight my hands; helping me connect deeply to the Divine while rooting me firmly on the Earth with an ancient remembering in my bones of what it means to be human. Thank you for helping me remember that the Holies always come first, for re-igniting my awe-muscle and for re-hydrating the deep knowing in my soul of how to be on this Earth in a good way. So many blessings on you.

To Ellen Tadd goes huge thanks for teaching me how to access wisdom—that sweet spot of knowing that transcends a thinking mind and a gut feeling. Thank you for sharing the wisdom of your guides, so that I too could access my Spirit—everyday in everyway! Your teachings inspire me to truly live as Spirit here on earth in human form, which makes life a whole lot more fascinating. And fun. So much heartfelt thanks, love and light goes to you.

And next…

To Mrs. Jean Slavin, my fifth grade teacher who told me I would write something great someday… thank you for planting the seed, for seeing my gifts and cheering them on.

To Rebecca Singer and Dr. Vimala Rodgers goes big thanks for telling me in no uncertain terms that I was supposed to be writing and publishing at this time.

To Janice Garrett—thank you for recognizing a soul sister and for your consistent nudge to get started.

To the friends and family who responded positively to the writing in my blog, so much thanks for nurturing the confidence to put my writing out in the world.

To "cold readers" Sandy Gascoigne, Kathleen Padulchick, and Lelija Roy, heartfelt thanks for the generosity of your time, your enthusiastic support and friendship, and your kind and helpful suggestions.

To my sister, Marie Kelly, who fed me delicious meals the first week of writing—thank you for nourishing my body, spirit and book!

To Adriana and Phil Christianson, who generously gave me use of their magical farmhouse in the final days to completion—so much thanks for providing the sanctuary I needed for the last push.

To my 2021 Wisdom for the Arts Community—thank you for being a steadfast container for my art, creativity and transformation, for being the push I needed to start this book, and for reminding me that creativity is access to the divine.

To Marci Shimoff, Dr. Sue Morter, Kim Forcina, Mary Garvey Horst, and my 2022 Year of Miracles Community—thank you for your year-long support to help me keep the intention of this book front, center, and alive, every day.

To my extraordinary book shepherdess, Marguerite Rigoglioso, so much love and thanks for helping me to anchor this book in both the earthly and spiritual realms, for holding my feet to the fire in a gentle and loving way, and for saying exactly what I needed to hear at the right time. You are a bright and playful light in this world.

To my editor, Richard Feit—my gratitude and thanks runs truly deep for your keen eye, your sharp intuition, your magnificent wit, and your playful spirit. You embodied all this with your marvelous competence, keeping the momentum moving while helping to shoo my nagging doubts away. Thank you from the bottom of my heart for making this book a reality!

To veteran book-guru Laura Shaw—my big thanks goes for your friendship and your time and tutelage, teaching me how the world of books and publishing and printing actually works. You gave me the boost I needed when creative juices ran dry and doubt crept in to rule the day. Thank you for helping me break the spell of inertia.

To editor Jaime Cox—thank you, Jaime, for putting on all the perfect final touches, literally at a moment's notice, along with your enthusiastic delight, which helped me take the next step.

I am so grateful to Mary Ann Casler-Brecher, the most amazing book designer I could have ever hoped for! You've made this process so much fun and I am so grateful for your intuitive creativity and wisdom, your steady patience with my endless futzing, and for helping me believe that my artwork is "good enough" to include in the book! I absolutely love what you've created.

To Penelope Love at Citrine Publishing who has created the most supportive, fun, wise and attuned process to birth this book. Penelope— you are such a bright spark in this world and I am so thankful for your wisdom, your deep intuitive sense, and your guiding hand—thank you for Being the Magic!

So much big Love and thanks, to the magical being who is my husband and fellow-adventurer in this life, Dave O'Donahoe—you are my strong and beautiful rock, and, fellow magic and mischief-maker. Thank you for your deep, steadfast, devoted Love and for making such delicious meals while I wrote.

And mostly—thank you to my soul who
just wouldn't let me sleep,
waking me up at 3 a.m. every day for a year,
until I started writing.

Diane Pienta

Writer, Mentor, Nature-Lover, Artist

"My life is devoted to Nature, Beauty, Creativity and Connection and in sharing their power with others—it's my way of creating peace in the world."

An avid spiritual searcher and playful student of life, Diane Pienta has always been a seeker of joy. Often wondering as a child "what could bring more happiness into this house?", her life has shown that play is anything but frivolous. It's a way into awe, wisdom, light and magic.

A cancer diagnosis in her thirties and adrenal burnout in her forties, following a high-powered track of Ivy League education and business success, led her to voraciously explore and experience what makes people love life and thrive, delving deeply into spirituality, human consciousness, herbal and energy medicine, alternative healing modalities, color, music and creativity.

Diane now pours her heart into writing, mentoring, and forest therapy guiding, devoting her life to Nature, Beauty, Creativity, and Connection, always in the quest to share their power with others. She hopes to spread seeds of peace and awe with her words and work, scattering them where they are needed most.

Equally at home fiddling or felting, painting or dancing, or gathering wonder-makers to cavort, frolic and picnic under a full moon, Diane reveres this magnificent world and loves to help others see and be their own light and magic.

When not off exploring new corners of the world and new ways of thinking, she loves living near the Muddy River in Boston with her sea-faring husband.

For more about Diane and further inspiration please visit:
www.dianepienta.com

Resources

I often learn about the most inspiring teachers, from other people. So, I'd love to pass some on to you! Here are some uplifting resources, mentioned in the book, that you might like to peruse along your journey:

- **David Abram** is mind-altering thinker, writer, and philosopher awakening us to our animal nature and what our true place in the world might be. You can find out more about David and his work with the Alliance of Wild Ethics by following the path blazed by his website; start here—wildethics.org/the-alliance—and follow the arrows to www.facebook.com/riverspell

- Forest therapy, according to the **Association of Nature & Forest Therapy** (ANFT) "is a research-based framework for supporting healing and wellness through immersion in forests and other natural environments." It is "a relational practice that brings people into deeper intimacy with natural places." ANFT's mission is to spread

the practice of forest therapy in a way that can help us feel alive, to '
fall in love with and care for the world in a way that benefits all
beings. Find a forest therapy guide here—or become one yourself.
https://www.natureandforesttherapy.earth

- The poetry readings and music of **Coleman Barks** will transport
  you to the enchanted. Google his videos. www.colemanbarks.com

- For over twenty years, the **Boston School of Herbal Studies**
  has been training herbal practitioners in an innovative, tiered
  apprenticeship program. www.bostonherbalstudies.com

- **Julia Cameron's** book *The Artist's Way: A Spiritual Path to Higher
  Creativity* is a must-read for reigniting and jumpstarting creativity.
  www.juliacameronlive.com

- The **John C. Campbell Folk School** is a transformative school of
  craft and community deep in the magical Great Smokey
  Mountains of North Carolina. www.folkschool.org

- **Robin Wall Kimmerer's** books are deeply soul-soothing reminders of how we belong to this Earth. www.robinwallkimmerer.com

- **Lynne McTaggart** has been researching the power of intention and how our thoughts shape our life for decades. Among her several books, *The Power of Eight* is groundbreaking and mind-opening. www.lynnemctaggart.com

- **Dr. Sue Morter**—Dr. Sue—teaches powerful, accessible ways to tap into our intuition and spirit. Her book, *The Energy Codes*, is a great place to start. www.drsuemorter.com

- Trying to tell you who and what **Martín Prechtel** is and does is like trying to describe the ocean; it simply can't be done in a few words. Martín is an extraordinary thinker, writer, artist, teacher, and story teller. In Martín's presence you can't help but remember who you *really* are and what's important in this world above all else. "I try to take everything that I do and show the people that they have an indigenous soul," Martín says. "There is a memory that is above the historical memory, deeper than the personal memory. It is the heartwood of the tree, in the bones." I highly recommend exploring his website, his books, and his school, **Bolad's Kitchen**. https://floweringmountain.com

- **Dr. Vimala Rodgers**, author of *Your Handwriting Can Change Your Life*, teaches how the way we shape our letters can shape the way we think—truly, the power of the pen! www.vimalarodgers.com

- Storyteller, mythologist and keeper/teacher of the mythic imagination, **Martin Shaw** can keep me spellbound for a very long time while I don't realize he's bringing my soul back to life. www.drmartinshaw.com

- **Spirituality and Practice** is a comprehensive website with all kinds of resources for spiritual journeys—films, books, art, blogs, and if you like, a daily email with a dose of wisdom. www.spiritualityandpractice.com

- Through his school, **Spring Forest Qigong**, Chunyi Lin teaches a wonderfully accessible, easy, and powerful method to keep our energy system vibrant and balanced. www.springforestqigong.com

- **Ellen Tadd** is an international clairvoyant and educator; her teachings are clear and practical and ring with truth.
  Her latest book, *The Infinite View*, is a wonderful compilation of her decades of teaching, a must read.
  Find her at https://ellentadd.com

Notes

Don't Try So Hard

Mary Morrissey, https://www.bravethinkinginstitute.com/life-transformation/programs/power-of-purpose (Brave Thinking Institute, 5 day Meditation Process), p. 18.

Failure is Your Friend

Caroline W. Casey, *Making the Gods Work for You: The Astrological Language of the Psyche* (New York: Harmony Books, 1999), p. 42.

Martín Prechtel, *Rescuing the Light: Quotes from the Oral Teachings of Martín Prechtel* (Berkeley: North Atlantic Books, 2021), p. 43.

Your Comfort Zone Will Kill You

Julia Cameron, *The Artist's Way: A Spiritual Path to Higher Creativity* (New York: Tarcher, 1992), p. 49.

Martín Prechtel, *Rescuing the Light: Quotes from the Oral Teachings of Martín Prechtel* (Berkeley: North Atlantic Books, 2021), p. 52.

"Let the Beauty You Love Be What You Do."

Jalal al-Din Rumi, "On Spring Giddiness," in *The Essential Rumi*, trans. Coleman Banks (San Francisco: Harper Collins, 2002), p. 55.

Paulo Coelho, (@PauloCoehlo), Twitter, November 9, 2014, 2:36pm https://twitter.com/paulocoelho/status/531530767323889664?lang=en, p. 55.

Jalal al-Din Rumi, "The Sunrise Ruby," in *The Essential Rumi*, trans. Coleman Banks (San Francisco: Harper Collins, 2002), p. 57.

Don't Wait for Perfection. Just Get in the Game

Tal Ben-Shahar, *The Pursuit of Perfection: How to Stop Chasing Perfection and Live a Start Living a Richer, Happier Life,* 1st ed. (New York: McGraw Hill, 2009), p. 58.

Reid Hoffman (@reidhoffman), Twitter, March 29, 2017, 10:46 a.m., https://twitter.com/reidhoffman/status/847142924240379904?lang=en, p. 60.

On Adaptability

Socrates is thought by most to be the most likely candidate for the quote, p. 86.

"The World Is Full of Lonely People Waiting for Someone Else to Make the First Move."

Epigraph: The Green Book, directed by Peter Farrelly (2018; Universal City, CA: Universal Pictures), p. 86.

On Wonder

Epigraph: Jalal al-Din Rumi, *The Masnavi*, Book IV, Story II, as translated in *Masnavi I Ma'navi : The Spiritual Couplets of Maulána Jalálu-'d-Dín Muhammad Rúmí* (1898) by Edward Henry Whinfield, p. 89.

E. B. White, Charlotte's Web (New York: HarperCollins, 1952), p. 91.

Focus on the Love Not the Wound

Tal Ben Shahar, *Happier no Matter What, Cultivating Hope Resilience and Purpose in Hard Times*, (New York: The Experiment Publishing, May 2021) and Permission to be Human YouTube (https://youtube.com/watch?v=4YHIA-96ZWg), p. 105.

.Transition Time

Larry Dossey, *Space, Time & Medicine* (Boston, MA: Shambhala Press, 1982), p. 109.

What's the Worst That Can Happen?

H. Jackson Brown Jr., *P.S. I Love You* (Nashville, TN: Rutledge Hill Press, 1999), p. 115.

Knowing Our Own Worth Is More Valuable Than All the Gold in the World

Joy Stone, *If I'm so Spiritual, why am I still so Anxious? How to Find your Center and Reclaim your Joy* (Lifestyle Entrepreneurs Press, 2021), p. 117.

"When You're Stuck in Dance or in Life, Take a Walk."

Title quote: Toni Bergins – Live Journey Dance experience at Kripalu Center for Yoga and Health, December 2015, p.119.

Patience Is Not Passive. Subtle Is Not Weak

Online Etymology Dictionary, s.v. "subtle," www.etymonline.com/word/subtle, p. 137.

"Shouting at a Flower Bud Does Not Make It Open Sooner."

Title quote, Christina Feldman, *T'ai Chi as a Path to Wisdom*, p. 139.
Carl Buehner, 1971 *Richard Evans' Quote Book*, p. 140.

Ask for a Word

Leslie Temple-Thurston, *The Marriage of Spirit: Enlightened Living in Today's World* (Santa Fe, NM: CoverLight Publishing, 2000), p. 145.

Become a Vociferous Blesser

Catherine Cowan uses this phrase although Thessalonians 5:17, "Pray continuously" is another common translation of this verse, p. 148.

"Stay in Your Own Lane"

Dr. Sue Morter, Year of Miracles 2022 online program January 18, 2022, p. 167.

Hospitality Is Food for the Gods

Henry J. M. Nouwen, *Reaching Out: The Three Movements of the Spiritual Life* (New York: Doubleday, 1975), p. 173.

Jalal al-Din Rumi, "The Guest House," in *The Essential Rumi*, trans. Coleman Banks (San Francisco: Harper Collins, 2002), p. 174.

"Give Something in Nature Twelve Secret Names."
Title quote: Martin Shaw, YouTube Video "12 Secret Names", November 23, 2018 https://www.youtube.com/watch?v=YZUV3HSoupA, p. 180.

Mark Twain, A Connecticut Yankee in King Arthur's Court (1889; repr. New York: Bantam Classics, 1981), p. 181.

"It's Never Too Late."
Nicole Lyons, Nicole Lyons Poetry https://www.facebook.com/nicolelyons-poetry/posts/whatever-it-is-that-stirs-your-soul-listen-to-that-everything-else-is-just-noise/2044097992514310/, p. 196.

Nature Must Be So Disappointed If We Are Not Dazzled At Least Ten Times a Day
Title: A riff on Mary Oliver's line "It must be a great disappointment to God if we are not dazzled at least ten times a day," from her poem "Good Morning," in *Blue Horses* (New York: Penguin, 2014), p. 197.

The Anxiety Is the Ego Trying to Assert Itself
Existential psychologist Rollo May is thought by some to be the most likely candidate for the quote, though it is variously ascribed to Viktor Frankl and Stephen Covey, among others, p. 200.

Don't Live like Nobody's Watching. Live like Your Ancestors Are Watching!
Title quote: Matika Wilbur, p. 202.

Everything in My Life Is a Gift—Everything and Everyone, No Exceptions.
Title quote: Vimala Rogers teaching the spiritual quality of the Letter G, *Your Handwriting can Change Your Life* (New York: Touchstone Books of Simon and Schuster Inc. 2000), p. 205.

Ellen Tadd, Monthly Meditation and Philosophy Class, Boston, 2017, p. 208.

"Let Us Give Thanks for Unknown Blessings Already on the Way."

Title quote: Quaker mealtime blessing in *The Whole Heaven Catalog: A Resource Guide to Products, Services, Arts, Crafts, & Festivals of Religious, Spiritual, & Cooperative Communities*, by Marcia Kelly and Jack Kelly (New York: Three Rivers Press, 1998), p. 208.

"One Positive Thought Creates Millions of Positive Vibrations."

Title quote: John Coltrane, John Coltrane Quotes – The Iconic Saxophonist in his own Words John Coltrane Quotes – The Iconic Saxophonist in his own Words, https://www.udiscovermusic.com/stories/john-coltrane-in-20-quotes/, p. 219.

What's Your Story?

Patrick Rothfuss, *The Name of the Wind* (New York: DAW Books, 2008), p. 231

Maya Angelou, *I Know Why the Caged Bird Sings* (New York, Random House, 1969), p. 231.

"Take Some Time from the Pursuit of Happiness Just to Be Happy."

Title quote: Martín Prechtel, Bolad's Kitchen teaching, 2018, p. 239.

Martín Prechtel, Bolad's Kitchen teaching, 2018, p. 241.

It's Time to Be Bold

Steven Pressfield, *The War of Art. Break through the Blocks and Win your Inner Creative Battles.* (New York, Black Irish Entertainment, 2002), p. 244.

A Final Musing

John Coltrane, John Coltrane Quotes – The Iconic Saxophonist in his own Words, https://www.udiscovermusic.com/stories/john-coltrane-in-20-quotes/, p. 245.

May the Magic Continue. . .

If I could bring magic to my life everyday, I would . . .

_____

_____

_____

_____

_____

_____

_____

_____

_____

If I could bring magic to others everyday, I would ...

_____

_____

_____

_____

_____

_____

_____

_____

_____

_____

_____

If I could bring more of my magic to the world, I would ...

_____

_____

_____

_____

_____

_____

_____

_____

_____

_____

_____

When I was little, the magic I loved the most was...